The Heartbreak Cure

Also by A.C Miller

The Vibrant Body
Reboot

The Heartbreak Cure

How to Get Over Your Ex and Move On in 48 Hours or Less

A.C Miller

ISBN-13: 978-1520229898

Disclaimer

This book is intended for reference purposes only. The author bears no responsibility for any consequences resulting from the use of information provided in this book. Please use all information at your own risk. Although it was created with the highest of intentions, the author can't make any promises as to its outcome. This book is not a replacement for professional therapy or counselling. If you continue to struggle with anxiety, sadness, grief or depression, please seek professional help as soon as possible.

10% of the royalties from the sale of this book goes to
The Samaritans – a free 24-hour counselling service
in the UK and Ireland

"And once the storm is over, you won't remember how you made it through, how you managed to survive. You won't even be sure whether the storm is really over. But one thing is certain. When you come out of the storm, you won't be the same person who walked in. That's what this storm's all about."

— Haruki Murakami

"Better to retire and save your aircraft than push a bad position."

— Goose, *Top Gun*

1.

Introduction

Break-ups can be horrible, wretched things. If someone meant a lot to you, and you invested time and effort into a relationship with that person, losing them will hurt like hell. No bones about that. And losing the future you planned together – that will suck, too.

You may be experiencing a cocktail of emotions right now – sadness, anger, fear, frustration, failure, resentment, loss, confusion, despair, grief, disappointment, anxiety, jealousy, stress, relief, desperation and guilt. You might feel emotions *about* the emotions – resentment at your anger, guilt about your jealousy, grief about your loss, and so on. You might also feel two conflicting emotions at the same time – love and hate, loss and relief, sadness and joy. Perhaps you have also lost your appetite and zest for life. Perhaps you feel numb. All of this can happen to the heartbroken, and can be incredibly difficult to deal with.

Humans are complex beings, with vast emotional intelligence. We can feel myriad things at any one time, and barely understand why or how. Grief is a very natural process, and we all experience it at one time or another. Sometimes the loss of a relationship can be harder to deal with than the death of a loved one because that person is still alive and well, we're just not with them anymore. This can be upsetting and hard to swallow.

Depending on the length and depth of a relationship, getting over someone can take anything from a few days to a few years. Some scars seem to never properly heal. There is a legend that says it takes half the length of a relationship to get over it. So someone you were with for two years would require one year to get over, etc. Another theory says the recovery period is directly proportional to the amount you invested in the relationship. So the person who doesn't really give a damn will probably walk away relatively unscathed. Whichever theory you subscribe to, one thing's for sure – when you're "in it", when you're heartbroken, it can feel like it will go on forever.

Well, my friends, I'm here to tell you that it won't, and nor should it. In fact, in just 48 hours you can make a considerable difference to the way you think and feel. You can jump-start your healing, then build on that progress and begin a new chapter of your life – feeling calm, free and fantastic.

Of course, heartache requires some sort of recovery period. I'd be lying if I said it didn't. It's important to honour your feelings and not bottle them up. Grief is an important emotion to acknowledge and express. But for some, heartbreak can drag on too long, and deplete both energy and spirit.

Whether they realise it or not, some people actually keep themselves stuck in its grasp by thinking and doing the wrong things. These things become habits. They feel comfortable. We hold on to the past, reminisce, wallow, get angry, maintain contact with the very person who's caused us trouble and pain. We indulge in daydreaming about our ex, and continue to be consumed. We don't want to do all this, but it's hard to stop. We then feel depressed and trapped, and can't see a way out.

It's a bit like being capsized in a kayak, turning over and over under water. You know you're under there drowning, but you hope that at some point you'll resurface downstream somewhere, and all this will be a distant nightmare. Which it will, because nature and time will take care of that. We metabolise grief slowly but surely like a big meal.

But wouldn't it be better if someone lifted you up by your life jacket today, and set you ashore right now so you can breathe again? This is what I aim to do in this book.

If you can become aware of what's going on, if you can understand the pattern of a break-up and work through it methodically and quickly, you can take back control and free yourself. It requires discipline, but it will worth it. Yes, you can let things take their own course. But you can also speed up the recovery process considerably by understanding it and applying some very practical and specific steps to leverage your way out.

Some people deal with heartbreak by going out and getting wasted and going home with the next person who looks their way. Others get into a rebound relationship, or try any number of knee-jerk reactions to make themselves feel better. But what will they learn? And who will they hurt in the process?

Chances are, if you do this, you'll be back in the same place in a few months' time, feeling the same way or worse because now you'll have a backlog of stuff you haven't dealt with yet, and new troubles besides.

Thankfully, there are healthier, faster ways to feel better and happier again.

Heartache occurs on the mental, physical and emotional levels, so in order to feel good again, we need to tackle all three at the same time to restore a sense of balance. The techniques in this book are designed to do just this – to heal heart, mind and body in unison.

Our thoughts dictate our reality, but our bodies also affect our thoughts. They're symbiotic. If we lie around all day wallowing, or if we abuse our bodies in various ways, then our thoughts will reflect this behaviour. Similarly, if we think negative thoughts, then our bodies are going to feel lethargic, angry and unwell. But if we heal both of them together, and maintain healthful thoughts and behaviour, then we will recover much quicker.

The brain is a very suggestible organ. If we work with it, if we use it to our advantage, we can make huge leaps in the way we think and feel. Our thoughts affect our reality. Using our imagination in a constructive way can make a huge difference to the way we feel, and therefore the reality we experience. You may have tried some of these techniques already. Others might be new to you.

I suggest you run through the whole book in 48 hours, then dip in and out of it for the following week. You might need to do some of the exercises a few times to get the full effect. But follow your own intuition and see what works for you.

You can do half the exercises one day, and the other half the next. Or run through them all in one day, then practice them again the next day. It's up to you. Once you've mastered a technique, you can then use it whenever you like, and you will have a skill for life.

I've also included a quick, 15-minute version of the *Heartbreak Cure* at the end, for when you have limited time or patience for the full course but need instant relief.

2.

The Aim of This Book

The aim of this book is to quickly get you to the point of not caring about your ex. How do you stop caring? You let go. How do you let go? You cut the addiction and attraction now, nip both in the bud, and at the same time create a present and a future that are so exciting and compelling they flood your heart and mind with hope and excitement about *new things and good things*.

This sense of newness is key. It acts like a magnet to draw you out of your present situation and catapult you into your brighter future.

When you find newer, happier, more exciting things to be doing and thinking about, they will naturally neutralise and eclipse any suffering and pain. And they'll make you feel alive again. Meanwhile, if you can pick out any valuable lessons from the past to apply to your new life or your next relationship, you will be way ahead of the game. What seems so awful right now can be turned into a positive. A big positive.

I've been through some pretty horrific break-ups myself, and at the time, I struggled to find the right resources and practical support to get me through. I didn't know how to cope so I reacted badly. In hindsight, I would have done things very differently. But at the time, I didn't know what or how. I often felt derailed, broken or depleted – like the sand after the tide's gone out. It took me a very long time to get over some people and piece myself back together – a bit like Humpty Dumpty.

So I began to find my own ways of coping. My own survival tactics. I devoured books, websites, blogs and courses. I gradually discovered all the theories and techniques you will read in these pages. I've included everything that worked for me, so you can recover immediately and not have to spend the same time I did feeling terrible. Nobody needs to waste any more time than is necessary. Life is too short and precious.

This is very much my own method. You might find another method works best for you – such as maintaining contact with your ex and weaning yourself off gradually. This has never worked for me, which is why I don't suggest it. But you are your own boss.

Also, it goes without saying that this book is not a replacement for good friends or therapy – I advise you to seek out both of these. What it will do is hopefully guide you through the dark times quicker and easier, so you feel supported, understood, and better in just a few days. Know that you are never alone.

If you follow all the exercises in the book, you should feel like a new person by the end of it. I hope these techniques work for you. I hope you will use this book like a friend.

Without further ado...

3.

What You Will Need

1. A calm and quiet space to yourself, without interruption
2. A few pictures of your ex
3. A few pictures of you and your ex together
4. A cardboard box
5. A good friend on standby (sometimes necessary, sometimes not, but nice to know they're there)
6. A scrapbook
7. A notebook and pen
8. Internet access

4.

What You Can Expect To Feel By The End

1. Relief
2. Peace
3. Detachment
4. Freedom
5. A renewed sense of hope
6. A renewed sense of self
7. Excitement about the future
8. Empowerment
9. New understanding

5.

The Ground Rules

For the purposes of this book, I'm going to assume you were the "dumpee", not the one doing the dumping. You didn't want the relationship to end, whereas your partner did.

If, however, you were the one who finished it, or if it was a mutual decision, you still might be grieving, so you still might find these exercises useful. But it will be a different kind of grief.

Before you continue with the book, I suggest you to speak face-to-face with that person to explain your feelings and your intentions before applying the no-contact rule.

Once you have explained how you feel, I advise you to keep a healthy distance from them to allow them to get over you. Please don't let your ego or any awkwardness or guilt get in the way of their ability to move on. Leave them alone to heal.

For the rest of you, I want you to agree to two very important things.

Rule No.1

The first is to stay away from your ex. This means no texting, no calling, no emailing, no Facebook, no FaceTime, no Snapchat, no back chat, no Viber, no Whatsapp, no random drive-bys, no hanging out in places you know they might be, and certainly no physical contact, especially on your own.

Getting over someone is a bit like coming off a class A drug. You need to go cold turkey. No quick shots to keep you going. Take a deep breath now and sever all ties. This is going to require courage, willpower and discipline, but it will be worth it. I promise.

All the healing that will take place within these pages will go on "behind the scenes" – that is, without your ex knowing. You don't have to discuss any of this with them. You need to create a little bubble for yourself in which to heal. Your ex will probably just sabotage this process and set you right back to square one.

Do not break the no-contact rule. It will be very tempting at times, but if you do, you will only undermine your own recovery, and fuel the addiction and attachment we're trying so hard to quit. If your ex does get in touch, simply ignore them or delete their message. Don't get drawn back in.

It might seem cruel to cut someone off, but it's necessary for now to gain some control, restoration and equilibrium. When we've experienced an emotionally charged event or trauma, our brains break it down into manageable chunks to digest and metabolise because it can't deal with the whole thing all at once.

By making a clean break and staying away from your ex, you give your brain (and body) the chance to process and recover, without drip feeding it yet more stress or stimuli. You might think you're being kinder to yourself by seeing or contacting your ex, but you're actually making your life and theirs much harder, and giving yourself more work to do. Contact will prolong the agony.

How can a wound properly heal when you keep picking at the scab (or pouring salt on it)? You need to be strong for your own sake, as well as your ex's. The no-contact rule is the most important one in this book. Plus, if you really and truly *are* meant to get back together, this time apart will be the deciding factor. If you keep holding on, how are you supposed to know what you want? How can you have enough space to work out if they're right for you? If you don't let go, you'll never know. I know this is hard, and *really* scary, but please trust me.

I'm not saying your ex is a terrible person, or you can never be friends ever again, I'm just saying that by giving yourself some distance, taking responsibility for your own happiness and future, and moving on gracefully and purposefully means you are far more likely to look back in fondness rather than agony.

The quicker you move on, the quicker you can be cool about it all. Maybe in a few months or years you can hang out as friends. But for now, it's *far* too soon. Trust me, at least one of you will still have feelings for the other. Which means at least one of you will have a hidden agenda to the meet-ups, and that can only lead to trouble.

Many people fall into this "let's be friends" trap because it's so tempting and so easy – and in many ways, makes complete sense. They say things to rationalise their actions, such as "it's childish to ignore someone, grown-ups should be able to be friends". But going from lover to friend is a slippery, potentially damaging slope. For both parties. No matter what age you are. It does both friendship and romantic love a disservice.

If you find out your ex is seeing someone new, all the more reason to let them go. Do not try and compete. Do not be the third wheel. Do not get angry. Do not pass go or collect £200. Detach and move on. You are too good to suffer the indignity of a love triangle. Wave them goodbye and wish them well.

"Ah, but I love them!" I hear you cry. "And if I let them go, they might never come back!" Well, my friend, if they don't come back, they weren't right for you. Hanging on to someone to try and keep them in love with you is a bad idea by anyone's standards. Plus, if you do truly love someone, letting them go and wishing them well is the kindest (and bravest) thing you can do. Be brave.

Letting go is win-win. If they love you, they'll come back. If not, you will have moved on to pastures new anyway.

Rule No.2

The second ground rule is to steer clear of:

1. Love songs
2. Romance fiction
3. Any coupled-up or married friends, especially if they try to give you advice
4. Anything that involves two people in a relationship or in love. Ban anything romantic or slushy from your life. Yes, that includes day-dreaming (unless it's about your fabulous future, of course).

Like the no-contact rule, this might seem extreme, but it's a temporary yet necessary step on your road to recovery. You wouldn't hang out in a bar if you were a recovering alcoholic, would you? Meeting up with anyone or anything that is in love will just highlight your loss and depress you further.

You're in a sensitive enough place, without making life harder on yourself. You need to be kind to yourself and enforce some boundaries while you build yourself back up again.

I appreciate all this might be very difficult if you have children, or if you have a very valid reason for maintaining contact with your ex. In these instances, I suggest asking an intermediary to help out. Someone you trust – someone who is calm, reasonable and on your side.

Also, if you have children, some of the exercises below might not be as possible or easy. They will require more thought and time. I also strongly suggest you see a counsellor or therapist, not just for your own sake, but for your children's too, because they will also be going through the separation, and will be acutely aware of all your feelings. Kids feel it all.

6.

The Techniques

I've made the exercises as simple, powerful and effective as I can.
The techniques are based on the best teachings of NLP
(neuro-linguistic programming), TFT (thought field therapy),
neuroscience, self-hypnosis, yoga, guided meditation, mindfulness,
feng shui, chi kung (Qigong), Reiki, Matrix Reimprinting, positive
psychology and life coaching. I've also included the lessons and
coping strategies gleaned from my own journey and experience.

Some of the exercises – such as the tapping sequence and breath
control – are especially good for any moments when, for whatever
reason, you're really struggling and need instant relief.

Remember to read through each exercise a couple of times before
you start, so you know what to do. And if something doesn't feel
right, just stop and move on to the next one. What works for one
person might not work for the next. And feel free to adapt anything
to your own needs. This is your book after all. But try and give
everything at least one go, and remain as open-minded as you can.
The more you practice, the quicker you'll feel better.

7.

The Pattern of a Break-Up

Let's look at the pattern of a break-up, so you can see where you are in the grand scheme of things, and work your way out.

Heartbreak actually follows a fairly set pattern, with people passing through different phases until they're out the other side. Of course, the amount of time spent in each stage depends on a variety of internal and external factors. And for some, the phases are interchangeable. You might feel anger *then* denial, for example. Or you might not feel any anger at all. Sometimes it can feel like one step forwards, two steps back. Every relationship is different, so every break-up is different. But as a general rule, the pattern goes something like this:

1. Shock and Denial
We often feel shock and denial when we hear someone has died, but we can also feel them when a relationship ends. Sometimes it's worse. We almost can't believe it. How can it be true? How can it be over? It doesn't make sense.

2. Anger
The next phase is anger. Once we've heard the news, we can feel furious about it. Our egos are not happy. We can feel abandoned and

rejected and think all kinds of horrible thoughts – about ourselves and the other person. Anger is a very natural reaction to a break-up, and it's important to honour and express it in the right way. There are ways you can release anger healthily and maintain dignity at the same time. I will show you some examples later in the book.

3. Bargaining

This third phase can be the longest because it's the one you can get stuck in. It's call the bargaining phase because it's full of false hope and games. You are still in love and attached to your ex, and you still believe there's a chance of rekindling the relationship. There has been no closure, no clean break. You try and win their affections by doing all kinds of crazy stuff. Whether they are drip-feeding you this hope, or you're doing it to yourself, you are still hanging on in there, and can remain so for a very long time until you cut loose and take control.

Unfortunately, some break-ups can be a long and protracted affair, and why I suggest you get really clear about what you want from your ex and from your own life, so you can nip this pesky phase in the bud. Grey areas only prolong agony.

4. Loss

In the fourth phase you have accepted the relationship is over. You may not know how to move on but you know you have to. This phase can also last a while, depending on the circumstances, and your own constitution.

5. Moving On

The fifth phase is when you are now getting on with things. Perhaps you've even met someone new or you're just happy being on your own for a change. You feel the relationship is most definitely in the past.

6. Freedom

In the last phase, you are completely free of your ex. They no longer affect you, they no longer matter. You remember them, but they're just a memory. You might even look back in fondness. But you have no attachment to that person anymore.

8.

_____

Your Tools

1. Subconscious
2. Habits
3. Beliefs
4. Associations
5. Hope
6. Imagination
7. TFT
8. Music

All the tools you need for this process are inside you right now. This course won't cost a thing (aside from the travel part, if you decide to do that), and you can do the exercises any time, any place.

You'll need some photos and other bits and bobs lying around the house, but everything else will be come from within you. Which mean you are in charge and in control.

Your main resources are your subconscious mind, your habits, your associations, hope and belief, and your imagination. All of these have the power to change your body's physiology and work for you or against you. By the end of this book we're hopefully going to have them to working *for* you. Here's how.

9.

Subconscious

Your brain is like a very powerful computer, capable of great things. Sadly, we don't use it to its full capacity, and often we use it to our detriment.

Put simply, the mind is divided into two parts – the conscious and the unconscious (also called the subconscious). The conscious mind is like the boss – the one that does all the active thinking, all the chattering away all day. It's the voice in your head running through your shopping list or making remarks about the person opposite you on the bus. Meanwhile, the subconscious mind is quietly busy running everything else behind the scenes, like a very diligent secretary.

The subconscious, which forms about 95% of your mind, is very good at taking care of you and keeping you safe. It keeps your heart pumping, your body running smoothly and you walking about without falling over. It's responsible for all your habits and automatic behaviour. Once it's trained, it's very reliable.

Anything you do on "autopilot" is a program running in your subconscious mind. But sometimes, these programs aren't very good for us, and they may actually hold us back. This book will help you reprogram your subconscious mind to get it working for you in a more positive way.

10.

———————

Habits

Most of our behaviour is habitual. We couldn't possibly think about every single detail all day – there simply isn't time. So we make generalisations and form habits to save time and energy. A habit is just something that's been logged at the subconscious level because it's been repeated so many times you no longer have to think about it. Repetition is key.

Habits can be good or bad. Your mind doesn't know the difference, it just logs it and runs the program.

When you're heartbroken, your habits are still very much formed around your ex and your old relationship. To change a habit, we must first become aware of it, then repeat an alternative behaviour until it replaces the old one.

It's a bit like walking through long grass over and over again until there is a new path. To make a new path, you just start walking a different route until the old one grows over again.

For example, any time you catch yourself thinking about your ex, immediately replace that thought with some of the benefits of being single, or focus on your ex's worst characteristics until that becomes the go-to mindset. I'll talk more about this later in the book.

11.

Beliefs

"Your vision will become clear only when you look into your heart... Who looks outside, dreams. Who looks inside, awakens." – Carl Gustav Jung, Swiss psychiatrist and founder of analytical psychology

Our beliefs form our reality. What we believe to be true about ourselves and the world around us colours our everyday existence. Yet we rarely take the time to examine those beliefs, and ask whether or not they still serve us.

Like habits, they have been logged and run on autopilot. And, like habits, they may or may not serve us well.

Beliefs can be limiting. If we believe certain things about the opposite sex, then that's what we'll notice, and that's what we'll always get. Our beliefs can become self-fulfilling prophecies. They can self perpetuate.

If we believe our ex was "the one", and we'll never meet someone as good as them, then we seriously limit ourselves and our future.

However, if we believe we can feel great again, and can be with anyone we want, we now have options, and our reality starts to shift accordingly.

Take a moment now to reflect upon your beliefs. Maybe you believe most people are fundamentally good. Maybe you believe the opposite sex is not to be trusted. Maybe you believe you're someone who is going to get married and have children. Perhaps you believe you're better off alone, or are just too independent, or will never find the right person.

Whatever you believe, just getting it all down on paper will help shed light on how you really feel about yourself and the world. Then you can see which beliefs are helping you and which are hindering.

12.

Associations

A lot of our habits are formed through association. We do two things at the same time and a connection is made. Neurons are fused together and will fire off more quickly next time around.

When we're in a relationship, we form lots of associations with our partner. We associate them with places, songs, films, clothes, smells, feelings, words, jokes, foods, colours, thoughts, feelings, anything.

These associations work on the subconscious level. Which means that, when we're not with that person anymore, our reference points are still attached to them. We often see things and experience things that remind us of them, or "only they will understand".

In order to detach, we need to break as many of these associations as possible, disrupt the neural pathways, and make new associations. This book will help you make the switch from old to new.

Keep in mind that a lot of people keep themselves addicted and attached to their ex by maintaining associations. They think about their ex all the time, they romanticise the relationship, dwell on the past, and hold onto things that remind them of that person – out of sentimentality, comfort and, quite possibly, fear. Letting go feels scary and lonely, and those old associations feel so right and so familiar, it's hard to shake them off. So the habits, and the neurons, remain strong.

The good news is, the subconscious mind is very suggestible so it only needs small changes, but if those are consistent enough, they become the new norm very quickly. Human beings love habits, but we are also very adaptable creatures.

What kinds of things do you associate your ex with?

13.

Hope

Hope, like belief, can be friend or foe. It can be a beacon of light, or a deceptive force. It can work with denial in a cruel loop to keep us stuck. Hope that's focused in the wrong direction, on the wrong things, can keep us stuck in a painful and frustrating no-man's land.

Sometimes we stay with people hoping they'll change, hoping we can help them, that they can help us. We can waste years hoping to get back together with someone, believing one day everything will return to normal, that they will see the light, realise the error or their ways and come running back begging for our forgiveness – "Oh, I was such an idiot! You were so right!"

But this rarely happens.

While there is still this kind of hope – false hope – there is no chance of moving on. We need to get real and quash hope now in order to fully let go and move on.

Ask yourself honestly:

1. What are the chances of getting back together with your ex and things being different?
2. How accurate is that hope? What hard evidence is it based on?
3. What advice would you give your best friend in this situation?
4. If you were on your deathbed, what advice would you give yourself right now?
5. What is true about this situation and what am I making up?

Hope in our own future is what we want to cultivate. Hope that moves us forward, gets us leaping out of bed in the mornings. Hope that puts a spring in our step and a smile on our face, not keeps us stuck in the past feeling unsure and miserable.

I once got over someone – despite being quite gutted about the break-up at the time – by reading Timothy Ferriss's *Four Hour Workweek* and making plans to start a business. The idea made me feel so excited that it completely eclipsed any heartache I felt.

Jot down a few things you feel hopeful about – things that don't include your ex. You can even write down that you hope you'll feel better soon, if that's as far as you can think right now. The more things you can feel hopeful about, the more lifelines you have.

14.

Imagination

"Imagination is more important than knowledge."
~ Albert Einstein

Our imaginations are incredible powerful, and they're our best friend for healing. Just by sitting still and directing our imaginations, we can make huge changes in our lives.

Much of the pain we experience in heartbreak is down to the way we use our imaginations against ourselves without realising it.

Neuroscience tells us that the human nervous system can't distinguish between a real and a vividly imagined event. So if we imagine something to be true, our bodies believe it to be true. We have a physiological response to our thoughts. Imagining moving your legs tells your brain that you are indeed moving your legs, and actually makes the muscles stronger – injured athletes and stroke victims have used this to build themselves back up to full health.

Similarly, the placebo effect is strong. Believing a pill will heal you does indeed help it to heal you. Thinking happy thoughts changes our brain chemistry so we actually feel better. Imagining the worst activates the fear centres in the brain so we feel scared and depressed. Thinking about someone strengthens the neural pathways associated with that person. Another reason why I advise the no-contact rule.

There is growing research in this area, especially concerning the use of creative visualisation to heal illness. But without a doubt, our mind and thoughts affect our bodies. The trick is to get them working in our favour (rather than our detriment). What you think, so you become.

The exercises in this book will ask you to use your imagination in very directed, constructive ways. This is to accelerate your healing, rewrite old behavioural patterns, and set you free.

The great news is that this movie theatre between your ears is completely free and private – no-one need ever know what you're doing. You'll need to set aside some quiet time, somewhere you won't be disturbed. Then you can access the creative visualisation state. This is also called self-hypnosis. You'll feel very relaxed, and can then imagine whatever you like to make you feel better.

Remember how, when you were a child, you used your imagination to create alternative realities? You could conjure up whole worlds that you believed in, and sometimes inhabited? Well, I'm going to ask you to do something similar here.

In each of the exercises in this book, I will ask you to imagine some scenarios and outcomes. Spend as much time as you can in each visualisation, and be guided by your feelings. The longer you can stay somewhere, the better. You'll know when the process is complete because you will feel a distinct shift in your feelings and in your body. You will feel lighter and happier. Then you can open your eyes and get on with something else.

15.

_____

Tapping

Thought Field Therapy (TFT) – or "tapping", as it's known – may seem like an odd thing to do at first, but it's hugely effective, and scientifically proven to work. Invented by American psychologist Roger Callahan, it stimulates the meridian and acupressure points that process trauma. And it's very easy to do.

Tapping can relieve pain, desperation, trauma, anxiety and any urges. It's deceptively simple, but once you've mastered the sequence, you can use it anytime, any place.

In this book, the tapping sequence can be added to most of the techniques to help process emotions and rewire your thinking. Think of it as a bit like the base for all the other exercises. But it's also the one to turn to when you're feeling any extreme emotion. For example, you might have suddenly heard from your ex, and be panicking or feeling angry or anxious. Or you might be finding it difficult to sleep. If you do the tapping sequence, you'll quickly come back to a calm and centred place.

Sometimes it's enough to just tap your fingers together or tap on your chest. Also, if you're not in a place where you can do your tapping physically, you can do it in your head instead – it works just as well (see previous chapter on imagination). Remember how our nervous systems can't tell the difference between a real and vividly imagined event? We can use this to our advantage here.

Here's the sequence as I learned it. You can do it on your right or left side, using your right or left hand.

1. Rate how you're feeling on a scale of 1-10, with 10 being the worst
2. Repeat the following phrase out loud, filling in the blanks: "Even though I feel ___, I deeply and profoundly accept myself." Repeat this phrase three times while tapping on the side of your hand, at the karate chop point
3. Focus on the negative situation or feeling as you run through the following sequence
4. Pat the top of your head 10 times with your hand
5. Tap just above your eyebrow 10 times with the tips of your index and middle fingers
6. Tap just below your eye 10 times
7. Tap above your lip 10 times, and below your bottom lip 10 times
8. Using your hand, pat under your arm 10 times, around four inches beneath your armpit. If you're a woman, it's right where your bra strap is
9. Tap on your collarbone, at the base of your neck
10. Then use both hands to gently tap around the chest area. Keep breathing, and keep focused on the negative feeling
11. Tap on the tip of your index finger
12. Tap on your collarbone again
13. Tap all fingers together
14. Now tap on the back of your hand on the "gamut spot", between your little finger and ring finger. While you're doing this, continue with the other steps
15. Close your eyes then open them again. Look down to the right then down to the left. Roll your eyes clockwise then

anticlockwise then close them again. Keep focused on the problem. Don't let your mind wander!

16. Hum the first part of a song, eg "Happy Birthday", which activates the right hand side of the brain, then count out loud from 1-5, which activates the left

17. Keep tapping on the back of your hand, between your fingers. Take a deep breath. Hum Happy Birthday again

18. Tap under the eye 10 times, and under your arm 10 times, then under your collarbone again.

Take a deep breath and notice how you feel. You should have reduced your negative feeling considerably. Repeat the exercise as many times as necessary to bring the feeling right down to a 1 or 2 out of 10.

16.

Music

"A screaming song is good to know in case you need to scream."
– Ruth Krauss, *Open House for Butterflies*

Music can change your state in a nanosecond. Try being miserable when you're playing your favourite song at full blast. Very hard. In this book, we're going to use this to our advantage.

Some music helps get rid of anger – useful at times when you just want to shout, scream or punch pillows. Other music makes you feel good. Feel-good tunes are a sure-fire way to kick you out of a funk and make you feel you can achieve anything again.

What we don't want is the sort of music that makes us go all teary-eyed, staring into the middle distance and pining for the past. No, no, no. Music is a mood-changer – use it wisely.

I'd like you to trawl your music collection (or online library) and create two playlists. One of feel-good tunes – songs to jump up and dance to – and another of screaming songs to punch pillows to. You know the ones.

I've created a sample mixtape at the end of this book to get you started. But yours might be different. Only choose songs that resonate with you, then blast them out while doing the exercises in this book.

17.

_____

Rhythm

We are energetic beings. Every cell and atom in the universe vibrates at a particular frequency. Our bodies are no exception. Bones, for example, vibrate at a lower frequency to blood.

In 1665, a study carried out by a Dutch scientist found that when two clocks were placed near each other, and the pendulums set at different tempos, sooner or later the clocks would fall into sync with one another.

The same can be said of humans. When we're in a relationship, we can fall into another person's rhythm. Their habits, their routines, their thinking, their vibration become ours too. In fact, the weaker object usually falls into sync with the stronger one.

Splitting up from someone can be incredibly disorientating because you've lost that very thing you were locked into time with. It can take a while to find your own rhythm again, to rebalance and recalibrate.

18.

Chemical Trance

We go through life in various trance states. The "in love" state is a particularly strong trance.

When we're newly in love, we tend to focus on someone's best bits and ignore the rest. The old "rose-tinted spectacles" come out and keep us from seeing the less attractive characteristics – or the wood for the trees. This is completely natural, and is thanks to hormones – a biological reason for us to pair up.

When two people fall in love, their brains produce chemicals that bond them together, mainly so they reproduce. Testosterone and oestrogen trigger lust. An increase in neurotransmitter dopamine means they are strongly motivated to seek reward and pleasure, ie, desiring and going after their partner.

An increase in adrenaline and cortisol causes sweaty palms and a beating heart, and sometimes a loss of sleep and appetite. A drop in serotonin can make them feel anxious and jittery and like they're going crazy. At the same time, oxytocin and vasopressin forge bonds and create attachment. It's a veritable cocktail of hormones. A real chemical trance.

Yet another part of the brain – the frontal lobe – actually shuts down. This is the part that controls judgement. Therefore, when we're in love, our critical faculties are severely compromised. This is why we can be blind in love. It also explains any extreme behaviour, both during a relationship and during a break-up. You're really not functioning normally!

If we want to fall out of love or lust, we just need to flip the biology around. We need to break out of the trance, sever any ties and attachment, create new habits, and only focus on the negative aspects of the other person.

Bear in mind, also, that a break-up is also a kind of trance. We only know how bad things were when we finally "snap out of it" and look back in wonder. Hopefully this book will help speed up that process, and wake you up from those trance states.

19.

Dignity

"Respond intelligently even to unintelligent treatment."
~ Lao Tzu, founder of Taoism

It can be very hard during a break-up, or in any emotional situation really, to not react badly. When we're hurting, and someone is pushing our buttons, we can respond automatically in ways we wouldn't be proud of later on down the line.

It's really important to do everything you can not to get caught up in petty squabbles or dramas and rise above it all. Any arguments, negative thinking and behaviour will only drag you back into the abyss, and take you further away from the freedom, peace and neutrality you're working hard to establish.

Try and remain as calm and detached as you can. This is one of the reasons why I propose the no-contact rule, because creating a bubble for yourself makes maintaining dignity so much easier. Don't put yourself in the line of fire – stay as centred as you can.

I'm not saying you should never express yourself or tell people how you feel. It's just it's better to do that from a calm and centred place. By now I'm hoping you will have said all there is to say anyway, but if not, think about writing a letter. It's much easier to articulate yourself in a letter because you have time to think and can't get drawn into a debate. You can say your piece without fear of interruption or conflict.

Of course, this goes against the no-contact rule, but if after a few days or weeks you're still bottling up important things you need to get off your chest, and if you don't say them then you can't move on, then a letter can be a good way of getting it all out. But only you can tell whether speaking out or staying quiet will be better in the long run. That's your judgement call.

It is possible to deal with a break-up gracefully. If you maintain composure now, you can walk out of this with your head held high. Go around throwing punches and slashing tires, and you'll feel stupid and embarrassed in a few months' time. Nobody's worth losing your self-respect over. Nobody. Yes, you might be a hot mess of emotion right now, but don't for one second act on that or reveal that to your ex. Deal with your own stuff in your own space, in your own time.

When in doubt, practice the exercises in this book. And if things get really bad, call a friend or see a counsellor rather than your ex. Ask your friend to remind you why you're not with that person any more. Having a friend on standby will give you vital support when you're feeling down. Sometimes it helps to go out and let your hair down, but just make sure it's in a safe place with people who love you, and nowhere near your ex. Having fun and feeling a release is great, but try not to do anything that will sabotage your recovery.

In a few weeks, once the storm has passed, believe me, you will be glad you created an iron curtain to recover behind. Break-ups are bad enough without adding embarrassment to the mix. In the not-too-distant-future, none of this will matter one iota, and you'll wonder why you ever got so wound up or upset. Trust me. Keep your cool, keep your head up and, as best you can, be graceful.

20.

Declaration of Intent

What I am about to teach you is a very powerful process, so you need to be ready for it. You need to set the intention now to get over this person fully and completely. By the end of the book, you will have drawn a line in the sand. No going back.

If you believe you can move on, and are committed to doing so, then sign the declaration below. Any sign of hesitation, and this process will not work. So only read on if you are truly ready and determined to fall out of love and let go of your ex for good.

If you're not willing to let go and move on, it might be a good idea to ask yourself why. And to find out what is holding you back, and if those beliefs and reasons are founded in truth, fear, delusion or wishful thinking. Please read the section on <u>Hope</u> and come back to the declaration when you feel ready.

I _____hereby declare that I am
ready to let go of _____ this very minute
and to prioritise my own health and happiness from now on. I am
committed to leading an amazing, truly fulfilling life, and I will let
nothing stand in my way.

Signed   Dated

CHAPTER ONE

AUDIT

EXERCISE: The Good, The Bad, and The Ugly

OK, we're going to start by doing an audit of your relationship. Getting things down on paper and out of your head will free you up to think about other, better things. Meanwhile, let's sort out the big mushy mess in there so you can think straight.

In your notebook, I'd like you to create three columns. In one, write all the good things about your ex – anything you enjoyed or appreciated about them or the relationship. All the happy memories and good times.

In the next column, write down all the bad stuff. Anything and everything you found unattractive or annoying about the relationship or the person. All the flaws – anything that springs to mind.

It might be the way they used to interrupt you while you were telling them a story, or it might be the way they snored like a ox at night, or perhaps they had an irritating laugh, or they patronised you, or put you down in public, or were always late, or they used to chew their food with their mouth open or fart in the mornings, in your face. The more things you can think of, the better. Be really specific here.

In the last column, I'd like you to write down all the benefits of not being with your ex any more. Jot down anything you can think of. Anything you no longer have to put up with, anything that frees you up. Perhaps you can now date that hot guy or girl in accounts, perhaps you can now move somewhere new, see your best friends more, enjoy more time alone, spend time on your dahlias.

You can add to these lists as more things occur to you.

EXERCISE: Old Exes – Where Are They Now?

Think of a time in the past when you were *really into someone* – an ex before this ex. How do you feel about that person now? Can you remember a time when you thought they were the best thing since sliced bread, and now you feel, what, *nada*? From this experience you know it's totally possible to get over someone – to go from head-over-heels to total ambivalence.

Write a list of all the people in your past who you were really in love with. The ones you cried over, talked nonstop about to your friends, thought about at night, and were convinced you were going to marry and live happily ever after with.

Next to each name, give that person a score out of 10 as to how you feel about them now. So 10 would be you are still totally in love with them, and 1 would be you never give them a second thought. This will serve as proof of your own natural ability to move on. If you can do it then, you can do it now.

EXERCISE: Benefits of Being Single

All things being equal, a relationship isn't always the right set-up for everyone anyway. Sometimes it is better to be single. We all move in and out of relationships as we go through life, with each status serving a purpose at the time. So why not embrace this time to be single? Because you never know long it will last.

Hollywood and romance fiction tells us we must have a soul mate somewhere, and if we haven't found them yet then, quite honestly, we haven't been looking hard enough. But maybe that's not true. Or maybe we have a thousand soul mates. And what constitutes a soul mate anyway?

Life isn't one big Disney movie. We come into this world alone, and we die alone. If you think your ex was "the one", perhaps all you have done is ticked "a one" off the list. There was a reason you met that person, a reason why you spent time together, and a reason why you broke up. Meanwhile, enjoy this time to be single! There's so much you are now free to do on your own. Think about it!

To get you started, here are some potential benefits to being single:

1. You don't have to put up with being unhappy with someone who doesn't value you/love you/adore you/give you what you want/make you laugh till your sides split.
2. No more compromise. Single people live life on their own terms.

3. Single people can go for whatever they want in life, without being held back by someone else, directly or indirectly.
4. Single people tend to exercise more. They have the time and inclination to keep themselves fit, they look after themselves better, they try harder.
5. Single people sleep better; no more sharing the bed with the old snorer/duvet-hogger/farter.
6. Married people often put on weight. Ever watched your friends get hitched then pile on the pounds because they're now "comfortable"?
7. There's evidence to suggest that married women are more depressed than their single counterparts. Maybe because they now have twice the work to do. Married men tend to be happier though, so go figure.
8. People in relationships often lose touch with certain friends or family members; single people make more of an effort, and are usually there when you need them. Thus:
9. Single people have more friends.
10. Being single means you can spend your money on what you want, when you want, and not have to justify it to anyone. You're in control of your finances. You can splurge or save, spend or scrimp.
11. Single people often have more meaningful work. They can focus their time and energy on their career and on what they want from it.
12. Single people have more time for themselves; they're self-sufficient and resilient.
13. Single people have more fun; they're more independent and can be spontaneous.
14. Single people can enjoy hobbies and nights out with friends without feeling a shred of guilt. They don't get pressured to stay at home to keep their partner company or (worse) do

chores. They don't have to ask anyone's permission to do stuff.

15. Single people can dash off on amazing adventures wherever and whenever they want. Then come home and make their married friends green with envy with their travel tales.

CHAPTER TWO

REMOVE REMINDERS

EXERCISE: Break-Up Box

I'd like you to find a cardboard box and place anything that reminds you of your ex into it. Photographs (bar the one you're going to use in a moment), letters, gifts, anything. Make things easier on yourself by eliminating all painful memories and reminders from your world. Objects and reminders will just keep you stuck, or worse, set you back. This will go a long way in helping to break the associations in your mind.

While you're at it, delete all texts from your phone. And delete your ex's number, just in case you're tempted to get in touch with them in weak moments. We all have them. Do this now and you won't do anything silly later. You can write down their number on a piece of paper and put that in the break-up box, if you must, but for now, just get it out of your immediate reach. You'd be amazed how many reasons and excuses you can come up with for "sending a quick text" or "giving them a quick call to see how they are" (note: how they are is they're trying to get over you, if they haven't already, so let them get on with it).

Make a separate folder for emails and set up an email filter, so if they do write to you, you will not know about it. Don't ever look in that folder. Not for a very long time, anyway. If you want, you can block their emails and calls completely. If you can't bear to delete their emails, print them out, and put them in the break-up box with everything else.

You'll feel a massive shift in energy just from doing this one exercise. Give your break-up box to a friend to keep safe, or hide it in the attic until you feel totally solid. Never, ever be tempted to open it.

EXERCISE: Book a Trip

"Travel brings power and love back to your life"
~ Rumi, 13th-century Persian poet

Travel is by far the best way I know to get over someone and to metabolise them fully. And in an ideal world everyone would have this option. Obviously not everyone does. But just going away for a weekend is better than nothing. Though, in my opinion, the longer the trip, the better. Going on a long trip/adventure is pretty much a cure-all for any woes.

Travel will give you much-needed distance from the things and people who bring you down, and will remove you from temptation and associations. Essentially, travel detaches you from the very thing that is hurting you, and at the same time fills the void with interesting and meaningful stuff. It's like a life massage and natural balm for the soul. It eases your pain on every level.

Seeing new things and meeting new people gives you new focus, new things to think about, new challenges, new memories. You won't have time to think about your ex or wonder what they're up to because you'll be too busy having the time of your life with amazing new friends. So what if they've met someone new? You won't care because you'll be in Bora Bora having a brilliant time.

And who knows when you might get another chance to spread your wings? Perhaps this time next year you'll be with someone new. You might even meet that person while you're away. So this might be your last chance to get out into the world and have a once-in-a-lifetime adventure. Use this time now to go out and have fun in the world while you still can. Today is the perfect opportunity to be free and feel free.

Is there somewhere you've always wanted to go? If you can't get a friend to go with you, why not go alone or book a group tour? Though I truly recommend solo travel. It's one of the most rewarding, educational, and life-changing things a person can do. You'll make lots of new friends along the way (who won't know anything about your ex or your history unless you choose to tell them) and they'll help you work through any problems or forget about them – whichever you wish.

Also, talking to new people will help you make sense of where you're at in your life. You'll get ideas and inspiration about what to do next. Ideas you could never have imagined if you'd stayed at home. Opportunities will present themselves.

By travelling, you'll also experience how the rest of the world lives, which will put everything into perspective and remind you you're in good company. Everyone has their ups and downs and challenges in life. Some more than others. And you'll be reminded that sadness and grief are universal. Everyone suffers.

Travel also gives you much-needed time to unwind and process, as well as the freedom to be who you want to be. In short, you'll become a lot more relaxed about stuff. You'll feel part of the human race again.

Although travel is my number one remedy for heartbreak, I'm not advocating running away from your problems. Not in the traditional sense, at least. Most of our problems come with us wherever we go anyway, so there really is no escape.

And some problems actually feel heightened when you're away. However, getting some distance from the problem gives it space to unravel and breathe. You'll be able to solve things much easier, and with clarity, because you won't be in the eye of the storm anymore. Things won't feel so complicated and raw when you're hundreds of miles away. You'll be able to see things for what they are. Many so-called problems will simply melt away.

EXERCISE: Change Your Surroundings

Now I'm going to ask you to change a few things around your house. It might be a full overhaul, or it might be something small, but the point is to shake things up in your environment. This is part Feng Shui, part NLP. Anything that creates something new physically will help create something new mentally, too.

You can do this before or after your holiday or trip, but I recommend before, so that you come back to a new scene.

My first suggestion is to move your bedroom around, especially your bed. Move anything that you spent time on or in with your ex partner. If possible, buy some new bed linen and redecorate your walls. Move your mirrors. Buy some fresh flowers. Do a deep-clean of your personal space.

If you've never heard of smudging before, it's an age-old Native American practice that cleanses the negative energy from a physical space to let new energy in. Dried sage leaves are burned and carried through the house – or you can buy an incense version, which is a bit less messy.

Even if you don't believe in smudging, try it for the sake of performing some kind of ritual. Rituals are very powerful, which is why they form part of all the major spiritual practices around the world. If you have the misfortune of still living with your ex, carve out your own space and maintain your boundaries until you or they move out. Then smudge the hell out of the place.

EXERCISE: Change Your Appearance

It doesn't have to be drastic, you don't have to get a tattoo or shave all your hair off, but changing your appearance in some way will help draw a line in the sand and create a sense of newness in your mind. Go to the hairdresser, even for just a trim, and buy at least one new item of clothing (even from a charity shop).

A new look is an easy way of signalling to your brain that things are different now. Smell is very powerful too, so if you can, ditch your old perfume, aftershave and shower gel and buy a new one. Remove any jewellery that has reminders of your ex, especially rings.

EXERCISE: Get What You Want

Break-ups can be messy, protracted affairs. The other person doesn't behave the way we want them to, they don't say the things we want them to say, they don't understand what we want them to understand. Argh! So frustrating. We can waste a lot of time and energy trying to get the other person to "see the light", be who we want them to be, who we know they can be if they'd just *pull their bloody finger out*. It's exhausting. At the end of the day, you can't change someone, or their behaviour. You can only change yourself. Sucks, I know.

A lot of the angst that stems from heartbreak is caused by us not getting what we want. So, before we go any further, I'd like you to write down in your notebook *exactly* what you want from your ex. Take a moment to really think about this, because it might not be obvious straight away. Imagine I have a magic wand and you can have *this thing*, which will absolutely become a reality. Perhaps you just want an apology, perhaps you want a proposal, perhaps you want them to tell you how much they love you. Perhaps – now you have the choice – you don't want to be with them after all. Really take your time to figure this thing out. Write it down in your notebook.

Now, once you know what you want, we're going to trick your brain into thinking it's has been given what it's been craving so it will calm the heck down. Run through the sequence below, and while doing so, visualise it happening for real. Let your imagination fill in the details. Don't worry, you'll still know the difference between reality and fiction, but your brain will have absorbed a more satisfying alternative and will therefore feel calmer. A bit like giving a child a lollipop to stop it screaming the house down. Let it have its way. Everything will be much easier once you've done this one exercise.

1. Run through a visualisation of what you want to happen in as much detail as you can, while you perform the tapping sequence below.
2. Pat the top of your head 10 times with your hand.
3. Tap just above your eyebrow 10 times with the tips of your index and middle fingers.
4. Tap just below your eye 10 times.
5. Tap above your lip 10 time.s
6. Tap below your bottom lip 10 times.
7. Using your hand, pat under your arm 10 times, around four inches beneath your armpit (if you're a woman, this is right where your bra strap is).
8. Tap on your collarbone, at the base of your neck, where you would tie a tie.
9. Using both hands, gently tap around the chest area. Keep breathing, and keep imagining what it is you want from your ex, as if it's happening right now. Go into as much detail as you can until you've really absorbed it into your body and mind.
10. Let your intuition guide you as to where to tap next. Sometimes you need to tap on your abdomen or back. But just be guided by your own body. Keep thinking about what you want becoming a reality.
11. Tap the tips of your index fingers together.
12. Tap around your collarbone once more.
13. Tap the tips of your fingers together.

14. Now tap on the back of your hand, on what's called the "gamut spot", between your little finger and ring finger. Stay focused on the visualisation.
15. Hum the first few lines of Happy Birthday and count from one to five.
16. Keep tapping on the gamut spot until you've completed the visualisation.
17. Take a deep breath in and out, and note how you feel. Repeat the exercise as many times as necessary until you feel satisfied you've got what you wanted and can now move on.

Dealing with rejection

Nobody likes to feel rejected. Our egos are very sensitive and can throw a full-on hissy fit when they don't get their own way. But we can choose how we deal with rejection. We can become a victim to our bruised egos, or we can take control, hold our heads up high and move on – their loss. In any case, who wants to be with someone who doesn't appreciate their amazingness? They've done you a favour by showing you they're not right for you.

Do not, for one second, try to win that person back or try to convince them how brilliant you are. If they haven't figured that out for themselves, that's their loss. Set your standards high. Do not stoop for anyone. Let that person go and see what happens next. They may or may not coming running back and realise the error of their ways. Either way, that's fine by you because you will be on to much better things, with or without them.

Refocus on *you* and *your future*. Rock your own life. They may or may not catch up with you. In time, if you play it right, they might wish they never let you go. But don't sweat it. You probably won't want them back by that point anyway.

As soon as you let go, a funny thing happens. The energy starts to flow again because you're no longer gripping on to something. And as the energy flows again, somehow people sense this and want you back (whether or not you take them is up to you).

EXERCISE: Turn the Tables

This is a useful technique to trick your brain into thinking *you* were the one who did the rejecting, not the other way round. It helps with letting go. It puts you back in the driving seat so you feel better and more in control.

Run through the tapping sequence above while following this exercise.

1. Imagine your ex is pursuing you. I mean, *really* pursuing you – sending you texts, presents, calling you at all hours, even turning up on your doorstep begging for you to take them back. I mean, *begging*.
2. Visualise all the things they might say and do to try and win you back. Don't go too far into what might happen if you get back together, we just want to bombard your mind with the idea of the boot being on the other foot – with you holding the cards, not your ex.
3. Keep tapping and keep going with this visualisation until you feel totally sick of your ex. Push it until you really can't stand them anymore.
4. Now imagine *you* have to do the rejecting. Perhaps tell them face-to-face to leave you alone. Whatever works for you and makes you feel most empowered and relieved. Go for it.
5. Keep tapping. Breathe. Phew. They're gone.
6. Note how you feel at the end of this exercise.

Checklist and Mantras

1. I've removed all objects, letters, gifts, reminders, texts and emails from my ex and put them into a box.
2. I've deleted my ex's number and contact details from my phone – or printed them out and put them in the box.
3. I've rearranged my furniture and cleansed my home and bedroom.
4. I've make a change to my appearance.
5. I've booked a trip to somewhere I've always wanted to go.
6. I no longer feel rejected. I am in control.
7. I'm feeling the beginnings of happiness and excitement.

CHAPTER THREE

SEVER TIES

These next exercises will totally change how you feel about your ex. They will help you detach and make you feel stronger and back in the driving seat.

This isn't about disliking or hating the other person. Nor is it about deleting any memories. It's about breaking the attachment, gaining control, perspective, distance, relief and peace – fast. So that you can be happy again. Because once you've detached you can actually think straight. Until then, you'll have a whole mess of emotions and ulterior motives going on.

The opposite of love isn't hate, it's indifference, and that's what we're aiming for here. Peaceful, respectful neutrality. All your memories will still be there, but the emotions attached to them won't be. You will still remember your ex and your time together, but you will no longer be obsessed or consumed by them. The pull will have gone. The addiction will be over. You won't care. If you bump into them in the street, fine, it won't feel like an episode of Jeremy Kyle.

If you can visualise a dial in your mind, with one side being love, and the other disgust, we're going to take your mind all the way over to disgust in order to break any current cravings or attraction. You'll be so turned off by your ex, you'll never want to see them again, let alone be intimate with them.

Don't worry, this feeling won't be extreme for long. It will level out to indifference very quickly. But we need to overcompensate first so we break the attachment and reach a neutral point. Then you will cease to care. Like you no longer care for someone you were in love with a long time ago. They're not on your radar any more.

So… are you ready?

What you'll need:

1. Your notebook
2. A picture of you and your ex together
3. Something that smells really disgusting, such as the kitchen bin or a full ashtray. Or if you have a good imagination, you can just recall the smell of something horrible instead. Maybe your ex's bad breath in the morning after a night on the town.

EXERCISE: Bad Memories

This next exercise is based on a powerful technique by NLP co-founder Richard Bandler. It's like a big old ninja kick to your attraction. After doing it, you will be totally turned off your ex, and will feel far more in control.

Focusing on the negative aspects of someone overrides any lingering attraction and addiction. And will have you seeing your ex in a whole new light.

1. First, take the picture of you and your ex together and write down how you feel towards that person now, on a scale of 1-10, with 1 being you feel nothing and 10 where you're madly in love

2. Now, put the photo down and close your eyes. Take a few deep breaths and relax. Recall a time when your ex did or said something to offend or upset you. Spend a few minutes running through that memory in your mind now. Make sure you are inside the memory, experiencing it first hand. Concentrate on how you felt at the time. Take your time with this. See what you saw, hear what you heard, feel as if it were happening all over again. How awful was it? Now magnify this feeling. What are you saying to yourself about this situation? Stay there for a few minutes until you feel really angry or repulsed

3. OK, now open your eyes and look around the room. Write a few notes about this memory in your notebook – where you were, what happened, what was said, etc. Number this experience "1"

4. Relax and take a deep breath. Put your notebook down and close your eyes once more. Recall another time when your ex did or said something to offend or upset you. Run through this memory in your mind now for a few minutes, focusing on how it made you feel at the time. See what you saw, hear what you heard, feel as if it were happening all over again right now. Magnify this feeling until it fills your whole body. Stay with it for a few minutes until you feel really turned off your ex

5. Now open your eyes, look around the room take a deep breath and write about what happened in your notebook and number it "2"

6. Repeat this process three more times until you have re-experienced five painful or negative memories when your ex upset or offended you

7. When you have five instances, and are feeling quite angry or upset with that person, take a look at the photograph of you and your ex together and rate out of 10 how you feel about that person now. The feeling should have reduced considerably. If not, revisit some more memories until it has. Try and get it to a 1 or a 2 out of 10. If you can get minus figures, you're doing great. If your ex was an absolute angel and never put a foot wrong, search harder or make something up

8. OK, take another big deep breath, and when you're ready, grab your notebook and remind yourself of those five painful memories again. We're going to sew all five together to form a sort of movie,

and run through it quickly in our minds, with no gap. So have your notebook to hand, and remind yourself of all five instances now.

9. Close your eyes and take a deep breath. Relax completely. Go back to the first memory, and play it again in your mind. Make sure you are inside the memory, not watching yourself from afar. Relive it as if it were happening right now. Then without opening your eyes, recall experience number two, then three, four and five. Run through them all back-to-back in as much detail as possible, as if you've cut a film of these experiences together without a break in between. Once you've run through all five, open your eyes and look around the room. How do you feel about your ex now? Rate it on a scale of 1-10.

8. Now, when you're ready, I'd like you to repeat this process one more time as quickly as you can. Then open your eyes, take a deep breath and look at the photograph. You should feel quite repulsed by your ex's image now, and not attracted to them at all. Keep hold of that feeling. Run through the process one more time, if you feel you need to, until you've extinguished any lingering feelings or attraction. Now take a big deep breath and do something else. Shake your whole body from head to toe!

OPTIONAL EXTRA 1:

Begin the tapping sequence as outlined above. Whilst you're tapping, go back to one of the memories in your list, and tap as you run through what happened. So you're inside your own body, in the memory, but you're tapping as you're remembering how awful it was. This time, however, I want you to do something different. Something you wish you had done at the time. Say whatever you wanted to say, and do whatever you wanted to do. Keep tapping.

Relive it now in the way you wanted it to go. Take your time with this.

When you're done, imagine walking away from your ex and going somewhere you feel happy and content. As you continue to tap, visualise friends and family coming up to you and giving you a big hug, so you feel safe and relieved. Keep tapping until feel a sense of relief and peace. Stay in this feeling for a while before opening your eyes and taking a deep breath.

You can revisit all five memories in one sitting, or come back to them later. The important thing is to take your time and feel the change inside you.

OPTIONAL EXTRA 2:

Run through the tapping sequence as you think about all that's good in your life, and all the fantastic things you're going to do in the future.

Each time you do this exercise, you rewire the neural pathways in your brain and detach further from your ex. Repeat as often as you can until you feel a change.

EXERCISE: Closing the Loop

1. Close your eyes, take a deep breath and relax. Go back to a time in your mind before you met your ex or got into your old relationship. Perhaps the day before, if you can remember that. Or any point in time that you can clearly remember. Create a picture of that moment in your mind. Spend a few minutes remembering this time. What were you doing? Who with? What kind of person were you? What was your life like? What were your hopes and dreams and aspirations? Make sure you are inside this memory. This is marker one.

2. Now, make a second picture in your mind of a time in the future when you've fully recovered from this experience and are happy and relaxed and enjoying life to the full again. Your ex is a distant memory. It can be any length of time in the future, it doesn't matter. Just as long as you feel totally free, and have moved on completely. Again, make sure you are inside this memory. This is marker two.

3. Take a deep breath and relax. Now, keeping your eyes closed, go back to marker one – to the time before you met your ex. Spend a few moments in this experience, then step out of it so you're watching yourself from afar.

4. Now, I'd like you to imagine that all the things that have gone on between marker one and marker two (ie, your entire relationship) have been recorded on film and you can watch everything now in black-and-white. Instead of experiencing it from the inside, from the first person, I'd like you to imagine you're watching it in the third

person, on a small screen in front of you. This will dissociate you from the experience so you feel less emotionally attached.

5. I'd like you to imagine watching all this footage of your relationship on fast forward, in black-and-white, with no sound, from start to finish. Maybe a few seconds' worth of film. Just whizz through from start to finish. Whether your relationship lasted two days, two years or two decades, just zoom through from start to finish.

7. Then freeze frame the last scene. Turn up the colour and the sound. Add in a feel-good soundtrack, make the picture big, and enjoy watching yourself happy and fulfilled again. Then step into the you that's on the screen, so you experience everything first hand. Feel as as if you were living that new happy life right now. Really let it seep into your body on a cellular level.

8. Now, after a few moments, step out of that picture and watch the screen again from the third person, as if you were watching a movie. Drain all the colour and sound and make the picture small again. From that last picture of you looking happy, I'd like you to fast rewind through your entire relationship again, in black and white with no sound, right back to the first picture of how you were before the relationship began.

9. When you get to the first memory, add in the colour and sound and watch it for a few moments before stepping in and reliving the you before you met your ex for a while. What were you doing? How were you feeling? Who were you with?

10. Float back out of the screen and watch this same scene from afar. Then, gently drain all the colour out of the picture, make it small,

remove the sound, and fast forward in black-and-white through the relationship to the final scene. Add in the colour and the sound and step in to experience it.

11. Repeat this whole process – stepping into the first and last scenes, adding in the colour and sound, then stepping out, removing the sound and colour and fast-forwarding or rewinding through to the end or beginning. It will take a bit of practice, but you'll soon get the hang of it. Just enjoy the first and last scenes, then zip through the relationship in black-and-white.

12. Once you've run through this exercise a few times, sit quietly for a few minutes. As best you can, clear your mind and take a few deep breaths into your belly. Open your eyes and look around the room. Make a note of how you feel now. You should feel very differently about your ex and your relationship. Repeat the exercise as often as you need to until you feel next to nothing.

OPTIONAL EXTRA

Imagine a big collage of your life filling the screen in front of you. Your relationship is just one small black-and-white square in the bottom right-hand corner. All the other squares that have nothing to do with your ex are in colour and make you feel happy. Shrink the picture of your relationship right down until it's barely visible. Then make it disappear from the collage completely.

EXERCISE: Uglify Your Ex

I think I might have just made up a new word, but it's the only one I can think of. When we think of someone, we remember how they look based on a mixture of images in our mind. A sort of visual shortcut, if you like. Usually, when we're in love, we see our partner in a favourable light, focusing only on their best bits. In this exercise, I want you to reverse this process. I want you to uglify your ex, on paper and in your mind.

1. First, I'd like you to draw an ugly cartoon version of them. Really exaggerate their worst features. Have fun with this. This might seem childish, but if nothing else it will make you laugh. By creating a silly picture and uglifying your ex, you begin to break down that old favourable blueprint and replace it with something entirely different. If you have good computer skills, you can take a real picture of your ex and digitally adapt it then print it out and stick it on your fridge. This, my friends, is a lot of fun, and very effective. Whenever you think of your ex, you'll now think of this picture instead.

2. Add a speech bubble next to the picture, and fill it with something annoying your ex used to say. Anything that used to turn you off. You can also add their list of annoying habits next to their picture to make it even more effective.

3. Now look at the picture while smelling something disgusting. Anything. Have a whiff of the drain, if you have to. But I also recommend old ashtrays and most things that come from a dog. Imagine that's what your ex smells like. Imagine that's

their breath as they lean in for a kiss. The combination of smell, pictures and words will form a huge turn-off, and act as a powerful deterrent to any lingering attraction.

4. To take this one step further, eat something disgusting as well – something that you really hate and you know will make you sick – then look again at the picture of your ex. Barf central.

EXERCISE: Lookalikes

This exercise is simple, but very effective. When you're dating someone, it's common to compare them with a good-looking celebrity, whether or not this is totally accurate. We all do it. However, the chances are that your ex also looks like someone not so good-looking. You have just chosen to see them like Russell Crowe or Brad Pitt or Cameron Diaz because, well, you loved them and it made you feel good. But perhaps they also looked a bit like your old geography teacher from school.

1. I want you to find an ugly or annoying celebrity, or someone else you know, who looks like your ex. This person cannot be in any way good-looking. In fact, the less attractive, the better.
2. Print off a picture of them and write your ex's name underneath. Stick this on your fridge.

For example, I once went out with someone who kind of, if you squinted, looked a bit like Tom Cruise. Well, once I'd made this connection, I couldn't think of him in any other way. In my mind, he WAS Tom Cruise. I bloody loved it. Then, the relationship went tits up, and I thought, right, who else does he remind me of, who I don't fancy? Gonzo from the Muppets, that's who. So I chose to think of him as Gonzo from then on, and that was that. Attraction over.

EXERCISE: See Your Relationship In
The Third Person

Any time you're struggling with painful memories, you can take yourself out of the picture and imagine watching actors or strangers in your shoes instead. This is called "dissociation". It detaches you from the experience and helps you gain much-needed perspective and distance. It also reduces any emotional attachment and feelings of victimhood.

1. In your mind now, play a movie of you and your ex together. What are you doing? How are you behaving towards each other? What's being said?
2. Now imagine yourself as a bystander, a stranger watching yourself from afar
3. What do you think about those two people over there? What are your impressions?
4. If you can remember a time when you were arguing with your ex, step out of the memory and imagine watching actors in your place. This should help detach you from the situation and reduce any negative feelings you have
5. How do you feel watching those people? What can you see? What would you like to see done differently? Replay it with these changes, if you like.

EXERCISE: Let Go

Zen Buddhists could teach us a lot about getting over heartbreak. The art of letting go is one of the hardest things in life, but one that is worth practicing and mastering.

We tend to hang onto things for fear of losing them, and often, the tighter we grip, the more that thing wants to leave us. If we can learn to enjoy it then let it go, the happier and healthier we'll be. But boy is this tough.

Most problems and stresses cease to matter once you learn to let go because most problems stem from gripping onto something. Hanging on creates tension, and tension creates stress. Energy can't flow where there's tension and stress. Nor can love. So letting go is more loving – towards yourself and others. The quicker you can let go, the quicker you will feel better and be set free.

As we tend to store a lot of our emotions in our bodies, especially our abdomen, this next exercise focuses on letting go from within our bodies. Because our body and mind are symbiotic, letting go physically will help you let go mentally and emotionally too. If you can do this once in the morning and once before bed, it's like a full-body MOT.

1. Begin by sitting or lying down on the floor with your arms and legs resting away from your body and your palms facing upwards. Bring your awareness to your breath for a few minutes.

2. Now focus on your left foot and relax all the muscles there – the toes, the ankles, the arches. Say in your mind "relax, relax, relax" three times.

3. Then focus on your right foot and relax all the muscles there – toes, muscles, arches.

4. Work your way up your legs, one at a time, breathing and releasing the tension in all the muscles – calves, knees, thighs. Each time, say in your mind "relax, relax, relax" three times.

5. Breathe into your belly and push it out like a balloon. Hold it for a few seconds, then imagine any pain or negativity releasing with the breath as you let all the air out through your mouth in a big whoosh. Say to your belly "relax, relax, relax" three times.

6. Focus on your chest and breathe into your lungs. Take in as much air as you can. Hold it for a few seconds then release any negativity out with the breath as you release the air through the mouth in a whoosh. Say in your mind "relax, relax, relax" to your chest three times.

7. Travel gradually up your body, relaxing each part as you go. Don't move on until you've let go fully in each area. If you feel any tension, focus your attention on it and breathe into it until it releases.

8. Relax the stomach. Relax the hips and the back. Relax the chest.

9. Focus on your shoulders and relax each one in turn. Each time you focus on a new area, breathe into it and say to yourself "relax" three times until you feel the release.

10. Focus on your neck, head and face, relaxing your eye muscles, your forehead, lips, scalp and cheeks.
11. Lie still for a few minutes and stay focused on your breathing. Say in your mind now: "I'm willing to release any thoughts, emotions and actions that no longer serve me. I'm ready and willing to let go now".
12. Stay quiet for a while before slowly getting up.

EMERGENCY EXERCISE:
For When You Can't Stop Thinking Of Your Ex

Here are some things you can do whenever you catch yourself thinking of your ex:

1. Freeze frame the thought, imagine pulling it out of your mind and throwing it away
2. Look at your mood board or vision board instead
3. Go for a run
4. Stand on your head, shake your body from head to toe, or attempt a complex balance or twist – it's very hard to think of anything else when doing these things!
5. Put on a feel-good song and sing along at full pelt
6. Practice making their image black-and-white in your mind, then really small, then fade it to nothing
7. Look at the cartoon character you've made of them and remind yourself of their bad bits
8. Make a list of things you didn't like about them
9. Make a list of all the negative memories or experiences you had with them
10. Meet up with friends who make you feel good
11. Watch your favourite comedy

Checklist and mantras

1. I feel far less attracted to my ex
2. I feel far less attached to my ex
3. I am able to let go of the things that no longer serve me

CHAPTER FOUR

DETOX

**"Be the silent watcher of your thoughts and behaviour.
You are beneath the thinker. You are the stillness beneath the
mental noise. You are the love and joy beneath the pain."
~ Eckhart Tolle**

During a break-up, or any time of emotional turbulence, we have a
lot of feelings to process, and these can be tiring. But if we don't deal
with them properly, they get stored in our bodies, and over time can
lead to ill health, even disease.

So it's a good idea to take the time now to check in and process
anything that's brewing. It's a bit like giving the garden a good
weeding – you want to regularly tune in to your body and mind and
keep them as negativity-free as possible. Developing the habit of
detoxing your system daily keeps you free of accumulated stress and
tension, and therefore less susceptible to illness and disease.

EXERCISE: Detox The Body

A lot of our feelings and emotions manifest as aches and pains. If we don't listen, or if we try and suppress or numb the pain with a chemical or substance, the pain will get stronger and louder until we're forced to deal with it, usually in more serious ways.

This next exercise is one you can practice each evening before bed. It's designed to help you release any pent-up emotions, such as anger, frustration, guilt, jealousy, anxiety and stress. It will help clear your system for a good night's sleep. It also ensures you never store up any stress or negative emotion, which can make you ill.

When we tune in to what's going on, focus on it and listen to it, it releases, and we can restore ourselves back to health and vitality.

1. Begin by lying on the floor with your arms and legs slightly apart. Relax and take a deep breath. Focus on your breathing. Tune in to your body. What's happening? What emotions are you experiencing? Are there any aches and pains or niggles? Where are they located? Scan your body slowly to feel what's going on.

2. If you don't pick anything up the first time, scan a second or third time until you do. Maybe you have anger festering in the pit of your stomach or in your shoulders, or sadness and twinges in your chest, or anxiety and a shortness of breath, or a heavy heart, or a headache or back ache. Whatever you feel, make a mental note of it, without judging.

3. Take one of these sensations and try to visualise what it looks like inside you. Perhaps it looks like green slime, or a heavy chain, or a red fire, or a cannon ball, or a tight band. Let your imagination guide you. There's no right or wrong answer. Really focus on the sensation for a few minutes. If you could pick it up, how heavy would it be? What would it feel like? What would it smell like? If there was a special box for it, what shape would that box be?

4. Relax for a while, then focus on each sensation in turn for a few minutes. Do this two more times – focusing then relaxing.

5. Thank the part of your body that is communicating with you today, and ask it what it's trying to tell you. If it could describe itself in one word, what would that word be? For example, tired, sad, angry, lonely, worried, guilty. Ask when that word entered your body, and what it is about, then listen to the answer. It might point you to a time in your life when you experienced the original emotion. But it doesn't matter if not. It might tell you what the solution is or what it needs in order to feel better. Just focus and listen.

6. Take a few deep breaths and thank the feeling. Emotions and feelings just need to be heard and understood, a bit like children. If we try and shut them up, they just get louder and louder. So thank your body for telling you what's wrong. Tell it you've listened and understood and are here to help and fix the problem.

7. If you can remember it, go back to the time you felt the original emotion, and remember what happened. If this feels

too much to handle, just stop and imagine writing it down on a piece of paper. Go back to your old self, or if it's a recent emotion, yourself today, and give yourself an imaginary hug. Comfort yourself, and tell yourself it's going to be OK. Use the tapping sequence to release the feeling and, if necessary, rewrite the old memory until you feel better.

8. Tune into that same sensation in your body. Now it's no longer needed, it can leave. Breathe into the area of tension. As you breathe out, say in your mind "release, release, release". Keep breathing into the area until you feel less or no pain.

9. If there is still pain or emotion there, stay focused on it and repeat the exercise until you have found the root cause and can let it out. You might find you want to cry or shout or punch pillows. Whatever you feel like doing, do it. Your body will tell you what you need. Or writing about it can be enough to excise the emotion, even if you simply write a few words in your notebook.

10. You may wish to seek counselling once you have identified what your issues are and where they are manifesting in your body. Sometimes just opening these things up and giving them air is enough to release them. Other, older or more severe issues, may take more time and attention.

11. Run through the body scan again until you've dealt with all the pains and hidden emotions in your body, one at a time. If that's enough for now, stop and do something else. Otherwise, continue with the next exercise.

EXERCISE: Surrender Box

1. Imagine you have a big box or sack next to your body. Take each emotion or worry in turn. Imagine what it looks like, then pull it out of your body and drop it into the box. Take your time with this until you really feel the release of each issue.

2. If it helps, you can visualise someone helping you – perhaps a good friend or family member, or someone you admire and respect. It can even be a character from a book, such as a fairy godmother or superhero. Anyone you like. You can also imagine them sucking the pain out of you with a tube. Or scooping it out with a giant claw. Whatever works for you! If you find it hard to imagine what the emotion or concern looks like, you can just visualise writing it on a piece of paper and putting that in the box.

3. Go through each emotion in turn until all of them are fully released (or written down) and placed into the box, then breathe a big sigh of relief. Now visualise your helper putting a lid on the box or sack, and taking care of it so you never have to see it again. The main point is to get this stuff out of your system and surrender it to the universe to take care of.

4. Once everything is gone, lie quietly and take a few deep breaths.

5. Now smile. Smile into your whole body, especially your mind and your stomach. Imagine thousands of little smiles travelling around your body and bloodstream.

6. Imagine a white light entering the crown of your head and travelling through your entire body. Make the light brighter and brighter until it fills the whole room. Bring the light back into your body then into a ball in the centre of your chest. Give thanks for all that is good in your life. Lie quietly until you feel ready to get up.

EXERCISE: Detox The Mind

Now we've detoxed the body, let's focus on detoxing the mind.

1. Start by visualising all the negative thoughts, memories and words that might have taken up residence in your mind. What do they look like? Picture them now. They might resemble red worms or brown blobs or mice. Again, let your imagination guide you. There's no wrong or right answer.

2. Imagine reaching into your brain and pulling out all the negative pieces one by one, like weeds. Imagine placing them in a box or jar next to you. You can actually mime this with your hand if it helps. Pick out anything you don't like – all the detritus and dross. Anything harmful or hurtful. Get it all out of your head.

3. Once everything is in the jar or box, Imagine flushing the contents down the toilet. Then take a deep breath.

4. Next, visualise turning on a tap at the very top of your head and feeling the cool water wash through your mind, flushing out any negativity or anything you no longer want in there. Feel the water wash all the way out through your feet, taking anything toxic with it. See the colour of the water turn from brown to clear as it cleanses.

5. When everything is completely clear, imagine breathing in a warm, golden, loving light up through your feet and legs, up

through your abdomen, all the way to your shoulders, then up to the top of your head. You can count with each breath, and watch the light travel upwards – one to your knees, two to your hips, three to your chest, four to your shoulders, five to your head. Bathe in this light and feel its healing energy working magic in your body and mind. You are now completely clear of negativity and instead are filled with healthy love.

6. Make this light so bright it fills the whole room. Then the whole planet. Then bring it back into your own body and mind. Feel its loving, healing energy.

7. Place your hands on your heart and think of five things to be really grateful for in your life. Dwell on each one for a few moments. Express thanks for each one in turn.

8. Now place your hands gently over your heart and belly and breathe softly for a few minutes. Your abdomen should feel soft and relaxed. Stay quiet for a while.

9. Note how you feel at the end of this exercise, and write down any thoughts or ideas that came up as you were doing it. If you practice this exercise throughout the day, or at least once a night, you'll feel much calmer, healthier and more centred.

EXERCISE: Monitoring Negative Thoughts

Automatic Negative Thoughts, or ANTs – can pop into our heads all day long. This is normal, but the problem is we tend to believe them and dwell on them. We think our thoughts are true. Worse still, we think they're actually *us*. When really, they're just thoughts, no more no less.

Our thoughts are very powerful in that they largely dictate our reality. So believing and indulging our negative thinking creates, well, a negative life. So we have to be very mindful of what soundtrack is playing between our ears.

As humans, we're supposed to be loving, peaceful and happy, but our thoughts get in the way of this *all the time*. If we believed half of what goes on in our heads, if we tipped it all out onto the floor, it would resemble a crazy, jumbled mess. To be at peace, we have to continually monitor our inner voice, and make a habit of catching it when it veers into negative territory.

Our thoughts have no meaning other than that which we place on them. And this is both liberating and empowering. It means we have control, and can listen or not listen. We can also change our thoughts and therefore change our reality.

The trick is to distinguish between the helpful thoughts and the unhelpful thoughts, and let the unhelpful ones go immediately, without giving them any energy.

It's a bit like sitting outside a cafe, watching the world go by. Our thoughts are like the passersby. We don't have to talk to the dodgy-looking ones or invite them over to join us at our table. But if some look interesting, spend time with them. Otherwise, let them walk on.

I realise this is not always easy or possible, but we can at least try. And the more times we try, the more of a habit it becomes. By analysing our thoughts and bringing them into the light, they start to lose their power and control over us. Instead, we start to assert power and control over them.

This is why the thought journal is so effective, because it forces us to not only monitor our negative thoughts, but to get them out of our heads and onto paper where they can be seen in the cold light of day. And where we can do something about them.

Then, by consciously substituting the negative thoughts with positive ones, our old habits can be broken and the record changed. We will have trained our brains to make the switch.

Any new habit takes a while to gather momentum and become the new norm. But it's worth the effort.

This next technique is part mindfulness, part cognitive behavioural therapy (CBT). CBT is popular among healthcare providers because it's measurable and gets results. It encourages us to evaluate our thoughts, not just automatically believe them. We can then brainstorm more helpful, optimistic alternatives. I've included a sample template for this process at the back of the book.

Next time you feel yourself going down the rabbit hole, stop, grab your notebook (or wait until you're in a place where you can do this), and try the following exercise:

1. Write down the negative thought. Copy out exactly what's running through your mind
2. Write down all the emotions you're experiencing with these thoughts, and the levels at which you're experiencing them. Exactly how are they making you feel?

Now I'd like you to look at what you've written, and ask yourself the following questions:

1. Is this thought true? How can I know for sure it's true?
2. Am I jumping to any conclusions here?
3. When I'm feeling happy, do I still think about this in the same way?
4. If a close friend of mine had this same thought, what would I say to them?
5. Could I have reacted differently here? If so, how?
6. Is there another way of looking at this situation? Brainstorm alternative, more optimistic ways to think about it. Try to come up with as many as you can.
7. How do you feel now? Do you still believe the negative thoughts?

EXERCISE: Dealing With Haters

"I will not let anyone walk through my mind with their dirty feet." ~ Mahatma Gandhi

For some reason, break-ups can cause a rumble of unfriendly behaviour from others. It's a good idea to have some tricks up your sleeve for dealing with these people, and for protecting yourself when you come into contact with them so you limit their impact.

Heaven forbid you have to deal with any haters, but if you do, here are a few tips:

1. Imagine you have a bubble, barrier or plate of armour surrounding yourself. This can be made of steel, concrete, glass or light. Any negative comments or actions just bounce right off your bubble and keep you safe inside. I sometimes like to visualise having Batfink wings that nothing can penetrate. Or a slab of concrete that I can simply hold up between me and whoever is trying to hurt me.. A friend of mine says she imagines putting on her space suit each morning and zipping herself in.

2. As best you can, try to avoid any arguments and conflict, and the people who cause them – either online, offline or in the street. If you must, say your piece calmly and succinctly, or take the high road and walk away. If you try and express yourself in the heat of the moment, or if other people are also

angry, your message will go unheard. When things are calmer, say what you need to say, then let it go.

3. Haters gonna hate. You can't stop them. Just pay them no mind, and walk away.

4. Draw funny pictures of anyone who's horrible to you, and stick them on the fridge to laugh at. Draw them with big ears and a big nose. Soon these people won't bother you because your life will have skyrocketed into amazingdom, but for now, just make light of them and laugh at them. They are probably suffering too, so don't pay too much attention to them.

5. Remember people who made you feel bad in the past – where are they now? How often do you think of them? Chances are they're long forgotten, as this situation will be very soon. Remember: in a hundred years' time, new people. Focus on yourself and your exciting life in the here and now, and let everyone else do their own bitching by themselves.

6. Dilute the negativity with positivity. If you have so much positivity in your life, people won't bother you so much because their poison will be neutralised by the good things you have going on.

7. Whenever someone says anything nasty to you, or rubbishes you in some way, immediately delete their comment from your mind, like you would on a computer. When you do your detox visualisations at the end of each day, weed out their

comment and flush it away with the other stuff you don't need. Delete, delete, delete. Reboot.

8. As best you can, do not take anything anyone says or does personally. What people say and do says more about them than it does about you. It's never about you really. Take solace in the fact that whatever they say or do hurts them more than it does you. They have to live with the themselves and their negativity, you don't.

9. Visualise throwing the negative comment or behaviour right back at the other person or throwing it in the bin – where it belongs. Sometimes I like to imagine leaving it on their doorstep, then walking away.

EXERCISE: Someone Else's Mouth

I sometimes like to visualise a celebrity or someone else speaking my thoughts out loud, perhaps in a funny voice or on stage to a large audience. This helps me detach from the thought and gain some perspective. Then I often see how silly it sounds coming from someone else's mouth. Or I know what advice I would give that person in my predicament. Try doing this now, and see how you feel after.

EXERCISE: Bla-Bla

When you can't shut your mind up, such as when you're trying to sleep, or when your thoughts are negative or someone has said or done something horrible and you can't stop replaying it, simply repeat the words "bla-bla-bla" in your head until it blocks out everything else. Try making it really loud, then a soft, kind voice. Play around with the tone and volume. It's very hard to think of anything when you're doing "bla-bla" and the negative thought has usually passed by the time you're on to something else. Or have nodded off.

TIP: Try using a word such as "forgive" or "off" or "repair", instead of "bla".

EXERCISE: Small Pictures

1. Think of whatever is bothering you right now and make a clear picture of it in your head

2. Take that picture, make it black and white, reduce its size, then imagine plucking it out of your head and placing it in your right hand. A postage stamp size is good, or the size of a pinhead

3. Now it's in your hand, not your head, look at the picture and hold it at arm's length and see how that affects your feelings. See how small and insignificant the picture is from over there

4. Now you can then either throw the picture away or throw it back at the person that's bothering you. You might also find it helpful to imagine hitting the delete button on the image, much as you would on a computer. The more you practice this exercise, the easier it becomes.

TIP: Try this whenever you catch yourself thinking of your ex. As soon as their image pops into your head, freeze frame it, drain away the colour and sound, and imagine taking it out of your head and placing it into the palm of your hand. Notice how it feels to have it there. Imagine crumpling the image up into a ball and flushing it down the toilet, along with any memories or emotions associated with the picture.

The more times you do this, the easier it will become. Then you will quickly form new neural pathways and a new habit.

EXERCISE: Eyes

Our eyes are closely linked with our brain activity. Practicing simple eye movements can stimulate the visual cortex and change our mood. If you're ever feeling overwhelmed, anxious or upset, try these exercises instead. Repeat as often as necessary.

1. Focusing on whatever is upsetting you, look from side to side quickly about 20 times
2. Close your eyes for a few seconds and relax. Open them and look up to the top, where a dark grey v-shape is. Hold this for 10 seconds
3. Close your eyes for a few seconds and relax. Open them and focus on the tip of your nose. Try and equalise your vision here for about 10 seconds
4. Close your eyes again for a few seconds and relax. Look from side to side again slowly, being mindful of going all the way into the dark space at the edge of your vision
5. Close your eyes for a few seconds and relax. Look from top to bottom 10 times slowly, as if you were drawing a straight line with your eyes. Keep thinking about the thing that was upsetting you
6. Close your eyes again for a few seconds and relax. Now, roll your eyes in a figure of eight pattern, five times one way, and five times another way
7. Close your eyes and relax. Staying focused on whatever is bothering you, roll your eyes once clockwise, then once anti-clockwise, reaching into the dark edges but not straining.

Close your eyes again and take a few deep breaths before opening them again.

8. Hum the first few notes of Baa-Ba Black Sheep then count to five. This will help disrupt the associations in your brain

9. Repeat as many times as necessary until you feel better.

EXERCISE: Breath

Learning breath control or *pranayama* allows you to feel calm and in control at will. It also clears your mind, focuses your thoughts and helps rid your body of stress and toxins, which build up in times of emotional turbulence. *Prana* means "life force" in Sanskrit, and *ayama* means "to extend".

Here are two really simple techniques you can try any time you're feeling overwhelmed or upset. I also suggest practicing them each morning and night to clear the mind and detox the system. Make sure you're wearing loose-fitting clothing before you begin. And if you feel out of breath or experience any negative sensations, just return the breath to normal immediately.

Breathing Exercise 1

1. Begin by sitting on the floor with your legs crossed. Relax your shoulders – imagine a golden thread lifting you up through the top of your head so you sit up tall but are also relaxed – like a coat on a hanger.
2. Now, make a fist with your right hand. Pull out your little finger, ring finger and thumb, and leave your index and middle fingers pressed against the fleshy part of your palm.
3. Lift your thumb up to your right nostril and gently press it closed. Take a long breath in through your left nostril.
4. Gently squeeze your nostrils shut using the ring and little fingers and thumb and hold for a couple of seconds. Then release the right thumb and gently exhale through the right nostril, keeping the left one closed.
5. Breathe in through the right nostril. Press both nostrils shut with the thumb and fingers and hold at the top of the breath, then release slowly through the left.
6. Continue in this way for a few minutes, breathing in through alternate nostrils. Aim for 10 seconds on the inhale and 20 seconds on the exhale, but just do what you can. As long as you breathe in slowly, hold for a few seconds and exhale slowly you will feel the benefits of pranayama.
7. If you feel dizzy at any point, stop and return your breath to normal immediately.
8. Any time you feel your mind wandering, just bring it back to the breath. Stay focused.
9. Take a few minutes to normalise the breath then repeat the whole exercise one more time.
10. Afterwards, drink a glass of purified water and sit quietly until you feel ready to get up.

Breathing Exercise 2

1. Lie down on the floor with your arms and legs slightly apart, in what's known as *shavasana* or "the corpse pose". Lie still for a few minutes to settle the breath. If you like, you can make a "mudra" by touching the tips of your thumbs and index or middle fingers together.

2. When you feel settled, take a long, slow deep breath into your abdomen, until it's completely filled with air. Only fill your abdomen at this point, not your chest. Take in a tiny bit more air. Hold it for a couple of seconds, then let the air whoosh out through the mouth. Relax for a few seconds to normalise the breath. You should feel your heart pumping.

3. Repeat this exercise one more time, this time imagining breathing in clean air and expelling toxins.

4. Now, take another slow inhale, but this time into your chest and lungs (not your abdomen). Take in a bit more air right to the top of the breath then hold it for a few seconds then let the air rush out through your mouth. Relax and breathe normally.

5. Repeat this exercise breathing into the chest, imagining breathing in clean air and expelling toxic air.

6. Lastly, take in a long, slow inhale through the abdomen, and once it's filled, continue to fill up the middle of the chest, then the top of the chest. Hold it at the top of the breath then release all the air through your mouth. Relax and normalise your breathing.

7. Repeat this exercise one more time – belly, mid-chest, top of the chest. Imagine how you fill a glass with water then empty it in reverse order.

8. Normalise your breathing. Then begin another round of three-part breaths, but this time clench all the muscles in your body when you get to the top of the breath, before releasing everything in one big sigh. Repeat this one more time before bringing the breath back to normal.

9. When you're done, lie quietly and breathe normally for a few minutes.

10. Now place one hand on your chest over your heart. In your mind, or out loud, say the phrase "I love myself, therefore..." and hear what comes next. Your mind and body will tell you the next part. Because you're calm and quiet, you'll be able to listen to your intuition or inner voice, which will always tell you the truth and knows what's best for you.

11. Listen to whatever it is telling you and acknowledge it. This will change each time you do the exercise, depending on your needs at that time. But it's a good idea to regularly tune in to your inner guidance and ask it what you need.

12. Ask yourself what is the best solution to the problem you're facing and again listen for the answer. When we relax and tune into ourselves, we receive the perfect answers. Thank your inner voice for its wisdom, and let it know you will take action immediately on what it has told you.

13. When it's time to get up, roll onto your side and lie still for a few minutes with your eyes closed. Push yourself up gently with your arms and sit cross-legged for a while before opening your eyes and standing up.

14. Make a note of what just occurred to you during this exercise. Afterwards, drink a glass of purified water.

Checklist and Mantras

1. I'm feeling clearer and lighter
2. I'm doing my breathing exercises at least twice a day
3. I'm doing a mental and physical detox each morning and night
4. I know what is best for me and I listen to my intuition

CHAPTER FIVE

SELF CARE

It would be very tempting during a break-up to eat junk food and get wasted every night in order to forget or numb the pain. But this will only make you feel worse.

As best you can, feed your body wholesome, healthy, nourishing foods, full of nutrients and natural goodness. Get plenty of good-quality sleep. Spend time with positive, nourishing people. People who make you laugh and feel good.

Get lots of love and hugs, read empowering books and watch uplifting films. If it feels right, wrap yourself in cotton wool for a bit until your heart feels stronger. Treat yourself with the utmost care. If you have the time and money, get yourself a massage, some Reiki or acupuncture.

Break-ups are emotional experiences, and we store a lot of that emotion in our bodies. Massage is a great release. Don't worry if you cry during your treatment. Therapists are very used to that! It's a good thing. Better out than in.

If you find yourself binge-eating or drinking, or waking in the middle of the night with anxiety or upset, run through the tapping sequence until you feel calm and centred again.

Rose essential oil is thought to relieve depression and anxiety. If you have a diffuser, add a few drops with some lavender oil to the canister and place by your bedside before you go to bed.

From a nutritional standpoint, make sure you're getting enough magnesium (which helps relax the muscles and promotes sleep), B vitamins and zinc, either through your diet or as a supplement.

If you're still struggling with stress, anxiety or cravings, try taking Sceletium (a native South African plant, which is a natural mood enhancer and eases withdrawal symptoms) or Ashwagandha – a traditional Ayurvedic remedy that helps the body deal with stress. Take both to help get you through the rough patch. For sleep, try Valerian, St John's Wort or Passiflora.

Yoga

Yoga is possibly the best all-round health practice I know of. More than just a series of poses or stretches, it's a whole integrated system of psychological, spiritual and physical wellbeing. Yoga eliminates toxins and stimulates healing. It also helps you feel grounded and calm, with a renewed sense of self.

For every hour of yoga you do, you also get an hour of meditation and relaxation thrown in for good measure. The more you practice, the more it transforms your body and mind in very subtle but noticeable ways.

A friend of mine once described yoga as "the art of forgetting", and in a world where our brains are bombarded with a million things to think about and remember every day, the art of forgetting is very welcome respite indeed.

Why turn to alcohol and drugs when you can do lovely yoga instead? I would recommend a daily practice for general health and maintenance, but up that during a separation, and any time you need extra support and strength to get back on your feet.

Please trust me on the yoga. If you've not tried it before, give yourself at least a month, then notice the difference.

EXERCISE: Mantras and Affirmations

Creating empowering mantras and affirmations that are personal to you works on your subconscious mind, and creates a shift in your mood and mindset. They also serve as a potent reminder to your brain of where you want it to go, and keep you on the straight and narrow whenever you feel wobbly. Play around with a few different words or phrases until you find something that really resonates with you.

It might be something as simple as: "I am moving on fully and completely with my life" or "I am free from worry and stress" or "I am positive and peaceful" or "I am feeling better every day" or "I only allow healthy and loving people and relationships into my life". Whatever works for you.

You'll know your mantra is right because it will feel good just to think it and say it. If it doesn't feel right to say it. You'll feel it on a cellular level.

If you don't fully believe your mantras, start small with a phrase such as, "My heartache is lessening. I'm feeling better every day". Then work up to something stronger.

I've included some suggested checklists and mantras after each chapter in this book, which are designed to be starting points for your own mantras. Use them and add to them as you wish.

Write out your affirmations and stick them on the fridge or keep them in your wallet. Repeat them as many times as you can throughout the day. Keep repeating them until you believe them and they feel natural to you.

If you use them with all the other techniques, you will be sending a very strong signal to your heart and mind, as well as the world around you, both of which will respond accordingly.

EXERCISE: Reiki

Reiki, like yoga, has subtle but noticeable effects on the mind and body. It's non-religious, and you don't have to "believe" in it. Like yoga, you just have to suspend disbelief and experience it. And the more you experience it, the stronger it gets.

As with yoga, it's freely available, has no side effects, is healthy and heals you where you need it most.

Here are the five principles of Reiki, as I learned them. Each morning and night, sit quietly with your hands placed gently over your abdomen or heart and repeat the following sentences three times each, until you feel a subtle change inside you. If you don't feel anything, don't worry. Just trust that it's working.

1. Just for today, I will not worry
2. Just for today, I will not get angry
3. Just for today, I will be kind to my neighbour and every living thing, including myself
4. Just for today, I will do my work honestly
5. Just for today, I will be grateful for all of my many blessings

Reiki is great for balancing energy and healing the body and mind. If you can't see a practitioner for a session, try this simple Reiki routine on yourself:

1. Lie still and place your hands over your eyes for a few minutes
2. Then place one hand over your root chakra (at the base of your abdomen) and the other on the third eye chakra (on your forehead)
3. Then move your hands to the heart and then the throat. Keep them there for as long as you feel is necessary. Let your intuition guide you
4. Afterwards, drink a glass of purified water and wash your hands. Do this morning and night

TIP: Try writing your own mantras in addition to the above. They might be "Just for today, I will forgive myself and others" or "Just for today I will let go" or "Just for today, I will be strong". Whatever feels right for you in the moment.

Checklist and Mantras

1. I'm taking good care of myself
2. I'm not allowing anyone to affect me negatively
3. I'm keeping away from negative people and situations
4. I'm learning about myself and creating strategies that work for me
5. I'm feeling more centred and calm
6. I'm practicing yoga and Reiki as often as I can
7. I'm feeling stronger day by day

CHAPTER SIX

FEEL BETTER NOW

As much as a good relationship, and a good person, is worth fighting for, I'm a firm believer in knowing when to bail. If you've tried your best to mend thing face-to-face, through counselling, or even in writing – and it's *still* not worked out, or is making you and everyone else unhappy, I'd take that as a sign.

I see no reason for sticking around to suffer some more. Yes, heartbreak hurts; but sticking around somewhere that's not working out hurts even more.

Society places a great deal of importance on romantic relationships, like they're some sort of badge of honour. But what might be good for one person might not be good for the next. And people transition between being single and being in a relationship sometimes many times during their life. One is not inherently better than the other.

Romantic love as an ideology is only a couple of hundred years old anyway. We actually don't need another person to "complete" us. We are enough. Yes, it's nice to have a best friend / soulmate / compadre, but it's just as nice to fly solo. That's what friends are for.

Commitment in and of itself isn't wholly good or bad. Commitment to the wrong things, to things that make us unhappy, can be highly destructive and lead to martyrdom and victimhood – and lots of other bad places you don't want to hang out. Many people in this world are committed to the wrong things, things that are bad for them, and far from that being cause for celebration, it's tragic and a waste of life.

Just like staying in a job you hate for 30 years is no great achievement, staying in a relationship that isn't right or good is nothing to be proud of either. It just shows you have the willpower and stamina for suffering.

Be discerning. You are worth more. Striking out and being brave and going for the things that elevate you and bring joy, even if that means being alone and scared and uncertain at times, is a far braver life choice. Be OK with being on your own. It's risky but at least you will die knowing you went for gold and didn't settle. How many people waste their lives on commitment to something that's fundamentally not right for them? Please don't be one of the body count.

There is a well-known story about boiling a frog. It goes like this. If you plop a frog into a pan of boiling water, it will immediately jump out to save its life. However, if you slide it gently into a pan of cool water and gradually heat it up, the frog will stay put – and slowly die.

Don't let commitment tip into martyrdom. Knowing when to pull the plug on something is a vital life skill. Far better to be single and temporarily heartbroken than shackled in gradual misery for the rest of your life. So as best you can, try not to beat yourself up for not being in a romantic relationship or for not committing enough. You did all you could. Now move on to better things.

Some say we are the product of our best decisions from five years ago. So you can tell what you were thinking back then because you'll probably be living it now. However, just because you made a particular decision five, 10 or even 20 years ago, doesn't mean it's suitable for you today.

It's important to keep reassessing your life and making sure your ladder is up against the right wall. Tune in and keep asking yourself if you're happy, and if not, why not? What can you do about it? What's working and what isn't? What makes you feel good and what's holding you back? Where will you be five years from now if you carry on the way you are going today? Is this where you want to be?

EXERCISE: Reframing

We've all heard of positive thinking, but it's easier said than done. When we're feeling down – in fact, any time, really – it's much easier to be critical than optimistic, especially about ourselves. We are our own worst enemy sometimes. And when we've just come out of a relationship, we can adopt a bleak view of the world.

But everything in life is just a matter of angle and perspective. Two people might view the same experience in totally different ways, depending on their mood, attitude or personal set of circumstances.

We can choose how we react to something instead of responding on auto-pilot. When we learn to actively reframe our situation, we can gain greater power and flexibility in our thinking, and therefore have more choices in how to behave. Instead of reacting automatically, we can come at a situation with resourcefulness, possibility and positivity. We are in the driver's seat.

What happens when we change how we view an event? Or the label we apply to it?

This next exercise will help you do just that, and turn the negative into positive until that switch becomes a habit.

1. Write down any negative thoughts you're having about your situation right now. For example: "I'm a failure. I never get anything right" or "I'm a commitment-phobe. I can't stick at anything".

2. Next to each thought, write a positive opposite or outcome. If it helps, imagine someone else has told you these things, and it's your job to flip them over to find the silver lining.

3. For example: "I'm a failure. I never get anything right" becomes "I try new things all the time. Sometimes they don't work out, but that's OK. Everyone fails on their way to success. Most of the time I do really well. The times I got it right were XYZ".

4. "Another relationship down. Why am I single again? Why do people always leave me?" becomes "One more relationship ticked off the list. This is great news. I'm one step closer to finding true happiness. Well done me".

5. "I'm a commitment-phobe. I can't stick at anything" becomes "I give things a go, but I don't suffer fools gladly. When things don't work out, I'm not afraid to walk away. I know myself well enough, and value my time too much to suffer. I am only committed to things that are good for me and that make me happy".

6. "I'm such a loser. This is miserable" becomes "I'm currently single. This is brilliant because I'm now free to do as I please for as long as I like and enjoy being me for a while, without compromise. This is the best thing that could have happened to me." You get the picture. Come up with as many as you can.

Exercise: Rewrite Your Relationship

It's easy to rake over the past and wish things had been different. "If onlys" are yet another cruel mind trick our brains play on us to keep us stuck and broken-hearted. We know we need to accept our past decisions and move on. We know we did our best at the time, with the information we had, and then. So why is it so hard?

Thankfully, we don't need to be stuck any more. By using the tapping sequence, we can rewrite any situations or moments in our heads. Again, it's like the child with the lollipop. We may not be able to change the past, but we can change our perception of it, gain power and flexibility, and move on feeling better.

If you are plagued by regrets, tapping and "reimprinting" can really help. In real life, things may never go according to plan. People may never understand, they may never listen, they may never say what you want them to say. But that's fine. In your mind, you can have it go however you like. Then you can let it go.

The following exercise is similar to Getting What You Want, except this one goes back in time.

1. Begin the tapping sequence – tapping the top of the head, above the eye, below the eye, above the lip, below the lip, under the arm, around the chest, the karate point on your hand, the back of your hand and tapping the finger tips together. Keep repeating this sequence as you continue the exercise.

2. Close your eyes and return to a time in the past that bothered you or upset you. Perhaps it was an argument or something you or your ex said or did.
3. As you remember the details, change them and have it go *exactly* the way you want. Say everything you wanted to say. Imagine the situation working out perfectly. Your ex listens to you, understands you, says what you need to hear. Play through whatever you wish to have happen in this scenario. Take as long as you like rewriting this memory, and keep tapping until you feel relief.

EXERCISE: Mood Board

Create a montage in a scrapbook or on a Pinterest board of anything or anyone that makes you happy (not your ex). This can be done on your computer or by cutting pictures out of magazines or collecting photographs, old-school style. Compile a visual log of all that's good in your life. Just as long as they have no association with your ex.

Pictures work very powerfully on our subconscious minds, and this board will serve to lift your mood whenever you're feeling down. Keep your board somewhere you see often, such as on your phone, on your wall, on the screen-saver on your computer. Look at it regularly, especially any time you feel sad, angry or upset, or catch yourself thinking of your ex.

Give thanks for all the wonderful things in your life, now and in the future.

EXERCISE: Vision Board

Now create another board of things you would like to attract into your life, such as a new partner, a new house, a holiday, new clothes, travel, a new job, particular items or experiences. I find playing upbeat music while I'm doing this really helps.

Once it's done, close your eyes and imagine watching a movie of your future. In this movie, you are living your life to the full, you're laughing and having a fantastic time. You are doing all the things you've ever wanted to do. Step into the movie and experience it first hand. Feel as if it's happening to you right now. Play the music while you do this.

It might sound strange, but the vision board *really* works. Anyone who's ever tried it will tell you that. I'm often surprised to see things on my board that have come true for me – in scarily similar detail. So beware – only choose things you *really* want to make happen!

EXERCISE: Gratitude Journal

"Gratitude is a vaccine, an antitoxin and an antiseptic."
~ **John Henry Jowett**

There has been a lot of talk about gratitude recently. It's become a bit of a buzzword. But this is because it's one of the most powerful ways to feel better and attract good things into your life. If you've never tried it, start now.

We live in a world where negativity surrounds us like amniotic fluid and it brings us down on every level and saps us of our joy. Complaining, criticism and pessimism are so commonplace, we don't even notice them anymore. Gratitude is the vaccine and cure.

Buy a new notebook today and start a daily gratitude journal, appreciation journal, thank-you-very-much journal, lucky-me journal. Call it what you like. The point is, you'll be retraining your mind to regularly focus on the positives rather than the negatives. And therefore that's what you'll get more of.

From now on, each night before you go to bed, I'd like you to write down the ten best things that happened to you that day.
Ten things to be really glad about. Or ten moments when you felt really lucky. When you write them down, feel as much appreciation and happiness as you can.

If you're struggling, scan your body and be grateful for all your inner organs, your eyes, your ears, legs, hands to write with, arms to hug with, a heart that's pumping, a voice that allows you to speak and sing. You get the idea. Soon, you'll realise you have hundreds of things to be happy about each day, and once you start noticing them, they will start multiplying. Admittedly, this takes a bit of practice, but once you get the hang of it, you'll start to see these things easily.

When you've finished that, you can look back over your life and be grateful for everything you've received – for your family, your education, all the food you had to eat, all the money you earned or were given, all your friends, your parents, your children, your home, your health, your memories, all the laughter in your life and the opportunities that have come your way. You can also appreciate just *being you*. Because you're pretty special. And that is worth celebrating.

Like your mood board, spend time with your gratitude/appreciation journal each day. Just a few minutes can be very powerful, I promise. Focusing on the good stuff will work magic in your life. Do it every day from now on.

TIP: An optional extra is to create a gratitude/appreciation/luck anchor by touching your middle finger and thumb together as you feel grateful about each experience.

Checklist and Mantras

1. I know there are many benefits to being single.
2. I feel more powerful and in control.
3. I'm taking care of myself to the best of my abilities.
4. I've created a vision board and mood board of things that make me feel good.
5. I have lots to be grateful for each day.

CHAPTER SEVEN

GET PHYSICAL

Break-ups affect us as much on a physical level as well as an emotional and psychological level. Not only do we store a lot of our emotions in our bodies, we've also been used to being physically close to another human being, and suddenly losing that intimacy can feel very strange and lonely.

It would be all too easy to slob about in our pyjamas in front of the TV. We've all done it. This is fine for a short while, but any longer and it becomes a slippery slope.

If we take care and nurture our physical selves during this time, in the absence of a romantic partner, we can alleviate many of these feelings, and process the loss quicker.

You may not feel like it, but try and take plenty of exercise. This will help process and eliminate toxins and stress, as well as release adrenaline and endorphins – natural feel-good chemicals. Plus, you'll look good and feel great, and you'll have tons more energy to get out there and rock your new life.

Exercise also oxygenates the bloodstream and stimulates the body's parasympathetic response, which makes you feel calm and more relaxed. This will help you to sleep better and heal faster. And it gives you something positive to focus on, especially if it's a team sport. As we all know by now, what you focus on, you get more of. So the more you exercise, the happier you'll be.

You can choose any form of exercise you like – it doesn't have to be a team sport, it could be a solitary activity or a combination of the two. The important thing is that you enjoy it. There's no point doing something you hate, just to get fit.

If you love dancing or swimming, do that. If you love golf, play a round or two each week. If you live for the surf, grab your board and take to the waves. And as much as you can, take long walks in nature. Surrounding yourself with nature and fresh air is a proven cure-all for most of life's woes. Plus, walking is great for processing thoughts and feelings.

EXERCISE: Power Pose

I got this idea from the brilliant Dr David Hamilton, who recommends doing a three-minute power pose each morning to set you up for the day ahead. But you can do it whenever you need a boost. Which means as much as possible in the next 48 hours.

Your mind and body are closely interlinked, so by changing your posture or moving your body in a certain way, you can trick your brain into feeling good. The more times you do the power pose, the more hard-wired confidence and happiness will become. You'll reinforce the neural pathways that make you feel good, and weaken the ones that make you feel depressed and upset. Use this exercise at least twice a day, and any time you feel down.

1. Put on one of your feel-good tracks at full volume. If you're worried about the neighbours, use headphones and lock yourself in the bathroom
2. Stand up straight, hold your head up high, plant a big smile on your face, puff out your chest, and breathe deeply into your belly
3. Then either hold your arms up in the air with your fists clenched (as if you've just won the World Cup), cross your arms over your chest or place your hands on your hips. Whatever feels most powerful and confident for you. Hold the pose for the duration of the song
4. Punch the air if you feel like it.

EXERCISE: Shake It Out

Whenever you experience a negative emotion – whether it's anger, depression or sadness – another useful technique is to shake it out. Put on some music and shake your whole body for a few minutes. Shake your legs, arms, hands, feet and head like a lunatic. Shake it out hard! You'll probably laugh at yourself. Don't stop until you feel better.

EXERCISE: Balance and Twist

Another good way to shift your mood is to try some balancing and twisting. Balancing helps calm your mind and clear your thoughts – try standing on one leg, or in the tree pose, or leaning forward on one leg with your arms outstretched. As you're balancing, you'll find it hard to think about other things.

Twisting is good for clearing toxins and tension from the body. In yoga, twists are important because of their cleansing benefits. Try sitting upright then twisting your upper body and arms round to look at the wall behind you. Hold for a few minutes before switching sides.

EXERCISE: Anger

"Raise your words, not your voice. It is rain that grows flowers, not thunder."
~ Rumi, 13th-century Persian poet

Sadly, we're not taught at school how to deal with our emotions and rid ourselves of negative energy in a healthy way. It's very unfortunate that emotional and mental health aren't more widely talked about, especially among men. We tend to store things up and then don't know what to do when things break down inside us and around us. We feel at a loss. We lash out or withdraw. My friend Ben once said to me, "The things that capsize us always happen on an idle Tuesday", and he's right. Often we don't see catastrophes coming. We can sleep-walk through life, thinking everything is OK, then one day, wham, we're knocked for six. If we don't have the right support structure and coping mechanisms in place, we can struggle to get up and dust ourselves down when life deals us an unexpected hammer-blow.

All emotions have a purpose, a positive intention. They're here to tell us and teach us something. Anger is one of the hardest emotions to deal with. It can cause sickness and disease and wreak havoc inside us and around us if we don't release it in the right way.

We get angry when we feel powerless, misunderstood, frustrated, threatened or attacked. Things haven't gone according to plan. Someone's overstepped the mark. The situation is unfair. Grrr.

Anger is like an internal weather system. It can be all quiet on the Western front then all of a sudden, a hurricane. Where did that come from? You can only keep it in for so long. And when it's out in full force, it can cause *a lot* of damage.

The thing about anger is that it can have many layers. You think you're reacting to one thing, but really you're reacting to multiple things – something else that happened to you that day, issues you stored up in the past and never dealt with at the time. Those are your triggers. Until you deal with the original issues, and process them as soon as they happen, you'll forever be reliving them. They'll always be triggered by similar events in future, usually with even greater velocity.

Anger is a useful emotion if we can understand its intention instead of letting it consume and control us. We need to find ways of releasing it in a healthy way, and not let it destroy us and everything in our path. When we feel anger, it's usually better to stop what we're doing, take a deep breath, and walk away from the situation instead of lashing out. This allows us to cool down and centre ourselves before tackling the issue properly and calmly, with the right frame of mind.

Following are some other ways to deal with anger.

Some Ways to Deal With Anger

1. Take a deep breath, step out of the situation and go for a walk or run (preferably in nature) until you calm down. Try and become a witness to the event and see if from all angles. Wait to revisit it with a clear head and deal with the situation or person calmly and quietly.

2. Go boxing or take up a martial art like Taekwondo or Jiu Jitsu. This will release anger and tension that can build up even on normal days. But one class when you're angry will do you the power of good.

3. Go dancing – either take a class, go clubbing or dance around the house. Dancing is one of the best feel-good forms of exercise I know. It's very hard to be angry when you're dancing.

4. Join a drumming group. Drumming has been proven to release stress and increase wellbeing. It's even been used as therapy for relieving post-traumatic stress disorder in war veterans. If drumming isn't your thing, just give the pots and pans a good whack.

5. Punch your pillow as hard as you can. Pillows won't yell back.

6. Yell in your car or alone in your house or in the middle of nowhere (but not at others).

7. Get an abdominal massage like *chi nei tsang*. Or massage your own abdomen, because we tend to store emotions in our stomach. *Chi nei tsang* can be a very powerful and emotional experience.

Expect to cry. But that's good. Don't ever feel bad about crying. Not ever. Crying releases tension and chemicals. Those salty tears do a valuable job.

8. Practice yoga. I recommend yoga for everything. It restores emotional balance, and builds your health, strength and fitness. It also helps you relax and eliminate stress and toxins. It teaches non-attachment and letting go. Yoga is a long-term method of healing, rather than a quick fix, so start now, if you haven't already, and in a few months you'll be a new person, I promise.

9. Sing. Sing along to songs that empower you and release stress. I've included a suggested playlist in the resources section of this book but sing to whatever makes you feel happy.

10. Laugh. Force yourself if you have to. But just laugh. You'll feel the endorphins release instantly. Laughter is a great medicine, and will relieve tension and improve wellbeing. Even if you don't feel like it, laugh as hard as you can. Any time you're feeling upset or angry, put on your favourite comedy and force out a chuckle. Build up a collection of laugh-out-loud clips for emergency situations like this. Also start writing down as many funny memories or things you notice during the day as you can. This can be from your own life or from films or books. Keep a note of funny things as they happen and add them to the collection.

11. Try a simple Reiki technique. Sit and place one hand over your third-eye chakra (your forehead) and another on your root chakra (your lower pelvis). Take deep breaths and stay there until you feel the energy has shifted. Reiki is high frequency energy, and helps dissolve anger.

12. See a counsellor and talk about any issues that are making you angry. Talking can help release pent-up emotions.

13. Write about how you feel, either in a journal, or as a piece of creative writing. Even a song.

14. Deep breaths. Practice the breathing exercises in the previous chapter to release your anger. Breathe into it.

15. Imagine watching footage of whatever is making you angry on a small black-and-white television. I like to imagine I'm in a cinema or theatre and the TV set is in the middle of the stage looking really small and insignificant. And I'm sat a few rows back in the pews. As I watch the footage of whatever is bothering me I sometimes imagine actors playing the part of me and whoever is making me angry. Then, when I get to a part that makes me really mad, I imagine good friends next to me jeering at the screen, laughing, and maybe even throwing tomatoes. That makes me feel a whole lot better.

EXERCISE: Chi Kung

This next exercise is based on the ancient Chinese art of Chi Kung (or Qigong). *Chi* means energy. Our bodies are full of *chi*, and this can become imbalanced during times of emotional turbulence or stress. Chi Kung aims to rebalance it.

A really simple way to feel better is to vigorously rub your entire body from top to bottom. This can be under or over your clothes, it doesn't matter. Start with your head and scalp, then move to your arms and torso, then your back, then each of your legs in turn. Do it a couple of times. You can shake out your whole body after this, if you like.

Now, standing with both hands cupped in front of you, take a deep breath, and as you do so, scoop up the air from the floor right the way up over your head. Imagine you're scooping up clean air and energy that cleanses you as it goes. When you breathe out, push your hands away and imagine pushing away any illness or negative energy.

Do this a couple more times until you feel much clearer. Now imagine a ball of white light in the centre of your chest. Watch it grow bigger and bigger until it fills your whole body, then the room and then the whole world. Stay here for a few moments before bringing the while light back into the room and letting it rest the centre of your chest.

Now imagine a bubble surrounding you, keeping you safe, shielding you from negativity, locking all the good clean energy and white light inside. Keep that feeling with you for the rest of the day and know that you are safe.

Checklist and Mantras

1. I'm releasing my anger in more mindful, healthy ways.
2. I'm taking plenty of exercise.
3. I know what to do when my emotions get the better of me.

CHAPTER EIGHT

LEARN THE LESSONS

"Sometimes we win, sometimes we learn."
– Gaurav GRV Sharma

I know it doesn't feel like it right now because you're in the middle of it, you're in the eye of the storm. But soon the storm will blow over, and all this will be a mere speck on the horizon. You'll still be able to see it, but you'll no longer bothered by it. It will no longer consume you. You'll be out the other side feeling stronger and wiser.

As the saying goes, "this too will pass". The important thing is to learn from the experience, take what you can from it, and leave the rest behind.

Every so-called disaster is a gold mine. If we can take the time to notice and take away the lessons, then things won't seem so bad. There is always a reason for everything, whether we're aware of it at time time or not. It's only when we look back that we can make sense of things. So trust that everything right now is happening for a reason.

Every person comes into our lives to teach us something, even the people that cause us heartbreak and pain. Even the worst relationships are full of lessons. Instead of looking back with regret and anger, if we can pick out those valuable lessons, we are always winners. This is something you always have control over.

It would be all too easy to get together with someone else to feel better about ourselves and ease our pain. And, sometimes, that works. We've all done it. But, without stopping to learn and evaluate, very quickly the old patterns will start to creep back in. History will repeat itself.

A lot of people go from one relationship to the next like monkeys in the trees. Their feet never seem to touch the ground. It looks like fun, but you know they're going to fall at some point and it will hurt like hell.

New partners can help us get over old ones and heal old wounds, but it's better to do that work ourselves. To learn and take stock, and create a solid foundation on which to build the next relationship. Otherwise we're forever plugging gaps.

Of course we all have a past, and we all bring our personal history to a new relationship – nobody is exempt from that. But it's unfair to dump all your dirty laundry at a new partner's door and expect them to wash it. It's not very fair.

So take this valuable time now to get strong and make yourself happy instead of looking for someone else to do that for you. You'll be a much better person for it.

EXERCISE: Benefit Finding

Benefit finding in a time of crisis can build optimism and a positive mindset. Sometimes, when we're in the grip of grief, we can think we've wasted time on a person or situation ("that's three years of my life I'll never get back" etc etc), but whatever we're doing, we're never wasting time if we're learning.

Use this time now to sift through the debris and take the valuables away. Write down anything you learned from your ex, from the relationship, and from the experience as a whole. Anything you're grateful for. Maybe you can only think of one or two things at this stage, but you can add to this list as time goes on. Perhaps your ex taught you how to make the best scrambled eggs in the world. Perhaps you learned the art of origami, or to be more patient or intimate or considerate.

Investment and sacrifice

Usually, the intensity and severity of a break-up will be directly proportionate to the amount a person invested in the relationship, and the mutual future together. So the one who did the breaking up has often emotionally left the relationship already, which is why they can move on so much quicker and more easily. They're one step ahead of the game. The one left behind has a lot of catching up to do.

If you sacrificed a lot to be in your last relationship – whether it was a job, a home, a country, family, friends, hobbies, values, beliefs, anything meaningful to you – the worse the separation is going to feel. You gave things up for someone who's no longer in your life. You may be able to pick some of these back up again, and I really hope you can. But sometimes we burn bridges when we're in the grip of romance. We get swept up in someone, and we let things slip that are important to us.

However, there is a very important lesson here to take forward into your next relationship. The more you give up to be with another person, the more you'll have at stake in the relationship, and therefore the more vulnerable and unstable you'll be.

If you've made a big sacrifice, or if you depend on your ex to fill lots of emotional, financial, psychological or social needs, it'll be pretty catastrophic if that relationship breaks down. Plus, it's not fair on anyone to expect them to be your "everything". It's just not healthy.

I'm not saying we shouldn't sacrifice *anything*, or compromise on anything, but there must be balance. If you keep some things back, if you're happy in yourself and rocking your life, you'll have solid foundations that will keep you strong if things go wrong. It will also make you more attractive and worthy of respect.

Really use this time *create your own* life and happiness before sharing that with others. And be discerning about who you let in. Commit to making yourself happy before committing to be with someone else. Make *you* your number one priority. For ever and ever, amen.

EXERCISE: Non-Negotiables and Deal-Breakers

Write down all the things you gave up doing, being or having when you were together with your ex. Write down the names of anyone you stopped seeing (either because you didn't have the time or because your ex disapproved of them), any hobbies or pastimes you let slip, anything you enjoyed that you did less of, any morals or values you compromised on.

Using that list, circle anything you are not willing to compromise on in the future – what I call the "non-negotiables" or deal-breakers. This will serve as a reminder next time around.

Write a few sentences to your future self. For example: "Next time I'm in a relationship I promise to put my health and friends first. I will make sure I get enough sleep and eat well. I will not stop calling my family and I will continue to go to my art class/football practice/knitting circle."

When we fall in love, we sometimes allow the relationship to consume us. We can lose a part of ourselves – or sometimes a lot of ourselves. That's perfectly natural, but the more we're aware of it, the more we can watch for it next time around, and not give so much of ourselves away. Then we're stronger in ourselves and within the relationship. We're less vulnerable and destabilised when things go wrong.

EXERCISE: Why You Got Into The Relationship

People get into relationships for a variety of reasons. Sometimes it's only partially because of their partner. Sometimes it's for another reason entirely.

The reasons might range from feeling bored, fed up with being single, a need for intimacy, sex, financial support, moral support, a child, a home, a friend, or something else that perhaps could have been filled in other ways, or by other people. This is good to know because it means we can find those things elsewhere – not necessarily by getting into another relationship – and thus remove much of our suffering and vulnerability immediately.

It also means we won't have to fall or lean so heavily on the next person we go out with because we will have learned to meet our own needs and spread our bets. Each time we conquer a weakness in ourselves, we gain more self-confidence and self-respect. Which helps us and everyone around us.

Take a few moments now to brainstorm possible reasons why you might have got into your last relationship, reasons that maybe had nothing to do with your ex. If there really weren't any, and you fell in love with that person purely for who they were, then that's fine. But try to be as honest as you can here. It's important to get things out in the open and see them for what they are, otherwise there's nothing to learn.

Now I'd like you to write down all your needs. It might help to look at Abraham Maslow's pyramid in the back of this book, which shows his "Hierarchy of Needs".

In his model, physical safety and health are the most fundamental needs for human beings, so they sit at the bottom of the pyramid. Self-actualisation and betterment are at the top because they depend on all the other needs being met first. Love and belonging can sometimes override the need for safety and physical health, as witnessed in abusive relationships and gang culture.

Have a think about your own needs, whether they're being met, how and by whom.

Once you've written down your ideas and answers to this section, brainstorm ways you might be able to meet your needs for yourself, without getting into a new romantic relationship. So, for example, if you wrote down social interaction or loneliness, you might write down that you'll make an effort to see your friends more, or meet new people, or get to know yourself and spend time with yourself until that feels comfortable.

You might decide to follow your passions and fill your life with things that excite and inspire you, or take up a new hobby, go travelling somewhere you've always wanted to go, start a charity, start a business, invent something new, write a song, write a book, study something inspiring, join a gym or club, see your family more often, or make new friends. Any number of ways to help alleviate loneliness. Everyone wants to feel loved, adored, appreciated, fulfilled and respected – it's only natural. But finding ways to fill ourselves means we won't always be relying on others, or just one person, to do that for us. And we'll feel much safer and more confident for it.

If you address the root causes of your behaviour, you won't start dating someone else – someone who might be wholly inappropriate – just to plug a gap or solve a pain point. Because then you'll end up back at square one, repeating the same mistakes over and over again. If our needs continue to go unmet, we will seek out ways to compensate, which can lead to unwise choices, or the playing out of the same old behavioural patterns over and over again. Take the time now to work out your needs and ways you can meet them.

TIP: Spend as much time as you can on this exercise, and come back to it as new ideas occur to you. Many of our limiting patterns are logged at the subconscious level so it can take a while to shine a light there and get everything out. Awareness is key. The more honest you are, the more you'll learn and grow. Be brave!

The Role of Parents

Whether we're aware of it or not, our parents play a very important part in how our romantic relationships look and feel.

As our first and most influential role models, our parents, and the conditioning we receive from them, is so strong, we hardly ever question it. And yet it's so deeply ingrained in our psyche, it affects everything we do.

On a subconscious level, our brains perceive our parents, and the way they behaved towards each other, as "normal". We don't question this because we're usually unaware of its influence, a bit like we don't pay much attention to the air we breathe. But it surrounds us and affects everything we do.

The conditioning is so strong, we often unconsciously look to recreate the same relationship our parents had, in our own partnerships. We copy the same patterns and dynamics without realising it. We look for a partner who allows us to play out these old familiar roles.

However, there's another dimension to this sequence of events. In a queer twist of fate, we don't always look for the other person to play the opposite gender parent. What usually happens is that we play the part of the parent whom we liked or identified with the most, be they our mother or father. Then we look for a partner to play the opposite parent. We don't know we're doing it, it just happens. Not all the time, but more frequently than we realise.

You might have noticed this pattern in your own life, or in that of ex partners or your friends. You might have even tried to help these people work through their stuff, or try to get them to change, only to hit a brick wall because the programming is so strong, so ingrained, it's too hard to change.

Think now about your own parents' relationship, and consider how they behaved towards one another. What were they like? Were they happy? Were they loyal and faithful? How did they communicate and behave towards one another? Who was the most dominant party? Which parent did you like or identify with the most?

Now think back to your relationships with the opposite sex and see if you can notice any similarities or patterns. Have you unconsciously recreated any of your parents' habits or relationship dynamic in your own life? Did it make you happy? Do you wish to continue this in future, or would you prefer to attract different kinds of partners or a different kind of relationship?

Bringing all this into awareness can help us break the spell. Then we can consciously choose what we want, rather than have it happen to us on autopilot.

TIP: I suggest talking this section through with a trained therapist because the conditioning can be strong and sometimes painful. However, the good news is it's never too late to make positive changes.

EXERCISE: Re-imagining Parents

Because our parents' relationship has such a big effect on us, re-imagining it can help us reprogram our minds so we can heal old wounds and choose the right people *for us*, not just the ones who perpetuate the same family cycle. This next exercise will help rewrite the script.

1. Close your eyes, take a long deep breath and relax.
2. In your mind, go back to a time in your childhood. Any time you like. Remember how your parents were with each other. Picture it now. What were they doing? What were they saying to each other?
3. Now, using your imagination, rewrite how you would have *wanted* it to be – in a perfect world. You get to be the writer and director of your own childhood here. If it helps, use actors or imaginary people in place of your real parents.
4. Watch your parents being kind and loving towards each other, as well as towards you. Play out a few scenarios. See them both as happy, content and fulfilled people, communicating lovingly and kindly.
5. You can also re-imagine your childhood home, if it helps. See any problems being dealt with in a healthy way.
6. Continue this exercise for as long as you can. Each time you do it, you can pick up where you left off and visualise another portion of your childhood until you've rewritten as much as you can. This won't change your memories, you will still have those, but it will rewire your brain to give you a new, healthier blueprint for what a good relationship looks and feels like.

TIP: Add in the tapping sequence for extra power. Tap your pressure points as you do the above visualisation and live your childhood the way you wanted it to be.

EXERCISE: Forgiveness

"Holding on to anger is like grasping a hot coal with the intent of throwing it at someone else; you are the one who gets burned." ~ Buddha

One of the hardest things to do when we're hurting is to forgive. Forgiving can feel like letting someone off the hook, as if we're condoning their behaviour somehow. But actually, forgiveness lets YOU off the hook. Hanging on hurts YOU, not the other person.

Forgiving is just another word for letting go, and we need to let go for our own sakes. This doesn't mean allowing someone back into our lives – we still need to maintain distance and boundaries to protect and respect ourselves. But truly forgiving someone *sets us free*. And freedom is what we want!

It is in our true nature to forgive. We know this because forgiving feels good, whereas hating and bitching feels rubbish. It's important to keep your mind and body as clear as possible. Don't let it get cluttered with bad feelings and resentment.

Because right now you really have four options. Staying with someone and forgiving them, staying with them and not forgiving them, breaking up and forgiving them, or breaking up and not forgiving them. Now we are in the latter camp, we are left with the last two options, and I know which one I'd rather choose.

Remember that the opposite of love isn't hate but indifference. If we hate, we are poisoning ourselves and the world. If we hate, we haven't truly forgiven, and we are the ones who suffer. We're still gripping the hot coal. Anger and resentment can fester inside us for years, eating us up, sapping us of our life force, and eventually causing disease. Therefore, it's paramount to let go as soon as possible.

So how exactly *do* we forgive? Well, there are many roads to the same destination. And what works for one person might not work for the next. Forgiveness can be very hard, but once we declare that we're ready, the process can actually be fast and transformational. We can:

1. Ask for help from the universe/your higher power/anything you believe in, if you like.

2. Create a meaningful phrase, word or mantra for forgiveness and repeat it frequently (such as "release", "finished", "forgive", "over", "free" or a phrase like "I am willing and ready to forgive and let go"). This will work on a subconscious level.

3. Writing and journaling about your feelings can help you make sense of them. Or releasing them in a more physical way – dancing, boxing, running, singing, drumming, painting, travelling, rock climbing, talking.

4. Doing everything we can to make ourselves happy. When we're happy, it's so much easier to let go and forgive.

5. Visualise yourself in the other person's shoes. This creates compassion. Imagine you grew up as them, had their family, friends, education and challenges in life. Then visualise yourself in your old relationship, dealing with you. This can really help give you some perspective and empathy, and appreciate why people behave the way they do. Everyone does what they do for a very good reason. By stepping into someone else's shoes for a few minutes, you can gain valuable insights into another's mindset, and therefore develop compassion.

6. You might also like to perform a symbolic ceremony. This can be absolutely anything, but it has to be meaningful to you. You could write names or experiences on Chinese lanterns and let them off into the night sky, write and burn letters, swim in the ocean, bury a box of things, light a candle and say a few words, write a song, whatever you feel has most symbolic value for the situation you are in. Symbolic ceremonies can be very powerful, and they needn't involve other people.

7. You could imagine going back in time and having a conversation with the person you're trying to forgive, to tell them how you feel and also apologise for any wrongdoing you are responsible for. You can imagine hugging them before walking away feeling happy and free. Take a look at John C. Parkin's book, *F**k It* and Louise Hay's book *You Can Heal Your Life* for more inspiration in this area.

All this goes doubly for forgiving ourselves as well as someone else. Because forgiving ourselves can be twice as hard. Go easy on

174

yourself. Give yourself lots of care and attention, and always, always, talk kindly to yourself. Monitor that voice in your head. Forgive yourself, forgive others, let go and move on.

Checklist and Mantras

1. I've learned the lessons I need to learn
2. I have a better understanding of my relationship patterns
3. I know what I need to do next time around
4. I have forgiven my ex, myself and anyone else that has played a part in my situation, and I'm ready to let it go
5. I feel calmer and wiser
6. I have brought my parents' relationship into the light and created a new blueprint for a healthy relationship for myself

CHAPTER NINE

CREATE A COMPELLING FUTURE

"What you think, you become. What you feel, you attract. What you imagine, you create." – Buddha

Now we've focused enough on your ex and the past, it's time to focus on the future and inject some much-needed happiness into proceedings. We're going to eclipse your heartbreak and pain with new and amazing stuff. Because the more you have to look forward to, the quicker you can move on.

Life is short and precious, and, although it may not feel like it right now, your heartache is a temporary blip on the map. In a hundred years time, none of us will be here anymore, and nobody will remember anything about this event. So live your life now! Dust yourself off and get back in the game.

There's a saying that if you continue doing what you've always done, you'll continue to get what you've always got. After a relationship ends, this can be the perfect opportunity to take stock and make changes.

Is there anything you've always wanted to do? Anywhere you've always wanted to go? Any outstanding goals or dreams to be ticked off the list? Write them down now! And get started on them!

Here are a couple more questions taken from the book *The Power of Full Engagement* by James Loehr:

1. Skip to the end of your life. What are the three most important lessons you have learned, and why are they so critical?

2. What one-sentence inscription would you like to see on your tombstone that would capture who you really were in your life?

Now think about the answers to these questions:

1. If a miracle had taken place, and you could be, do or have anything in the world, what would you be, do and have?
2. What would your ideal day look like?
3. Who are you when you're at your happiest?
4. If you carry on doing what you're doing now, where will you be in five years' time?
5. What do you need to do to become the best version of yourself?

EXERCISE: Top 10

"The best time to plant a tree was 20 years ago.
The second best time is now."
– Chinese proverb

Write down 10 things that you would like to do before you die.
A sort of bucket list, if you will. You can be as outlandish as you
like. Really let your imagination run wild. We're not looking to edit
this or work out how to make it happen, we just want to get it down
on paper and give our minds free rein to explore possibilities.

Try not to limit yourself to your current circumstances either.
If you live in one place but have always dreamed of living in
another, write that down. Or if you work in a certain industry but
have always wanted to do something else, get that on the list. If
you've wanted to travel somewhere, or study something, or meet a
famous person, or date a certain somebody, put that down, too.

Now imagine I have a magic wand and can make all 10 of these
dreams come true. Just suspend belief for a second. Imagine
everything has come true.

Now imagine I have shrunk all 10 of these wishes to the size of tiny
dots and placed them all in the palm of your hand. How do they feel
there, having all been accomplished? Just allow your brain to soak
up this idea before moving on.

Now, pick one of the goals or dreams on the list, and brainstorm how you might make it happen in the real world. Think of anyone who might be able to help you, any resources you have access to, any steps you can take to make progress. Break the goal or dream down into manageable chunks. What would be the first step?

This should feel exciting and challenging, not terrifying or impossible. If you like, you can write a date next to your goal of when you would like to have reached it. It's powerful to give goals timeframes. Write down a few words about how you will feel once you have achieved the goal. Focusing on how you'll feel will give your brain the motivation and target it needs to get you there.

Now, reverse engineer your goal to the present day. Work out all the small steps you need to take, and set deadlines for each one. So, for example, perhaps today you need to send one email or make one phone-call or do one piece of research. Then tomorrow you might need to make two more phone calls, or book yourself onto something, or meet with someone to discuss something. Keep going until you have created a plan of action for reaching your goal.

Once you have one mapped out, try some of the others. Don't worry if you can't plan them all out. It's enough to have them written down and to give your mind possibilities. You might also like to hire a life coach or mentor to help you. You're far more likely to achieve something if you have someone you're accountable to. Note how you feel at the end of this exercise. You should be feeling much more positive and hopeful about your future. If not, you're not working on the right goals for you! Revisit this section to work out what it is exactly that would make you excited to get up in the mornings.

TIP: Playing your feel-good songs while you do this exercise will help you feel positive and stay motivated

EXERCISE: In Five Years

Create an ideal scene for five years' time. What do you want to be doing? Who with? How will you feel? Fill in as much detail as possible. Build up a rich sensory picture. Be sure to include what you can see, hear, smell and touch.

You might be with a new partner, looking really happy. Or you might be scuba diving somewhere exotic, or dancing the tango in Buenos Aires, or laughing with friends in your new house. Whatever you like. Again, play your feel-good tracks, if that helps get you in the mood.

Stay focused on this scene for a few minutes, then express thanks for it and let it go. This acts as a sort of subconscious blueprint for where you want to go. Now all you need to do is trust that all this will happen at its own pace.

EXERCISE: This Time Next Year

Repeat the exercise above but for this time next year. Ideally, what will you be doing? Who with? How will you be feeling?

EXERCISE: Good Stuff

Make a note of all the things you love doing, all the people whose company you enjoy, anything that makes you happy. Grab your calendar or diary, and schedule in at least one of these things every day for the next two weeks. Ideally, do as many as you can. But if you can't manage it, do one thing a day as the minimum.

EXERCISE: Values

Just as your goals will be your targets, your values will be your
waymarkers. Goals can shift as time goes on, as our priorities
change, but values will tell you when you're off-course on a daily
basis. Take a moment now to write down 10 of your core values.
These will serve as a reminder of what's important to you – in
relationships and in life – so even if your goals change, or you meet
someone new, or feel a bit lost, you'll always know you're on the
right path in yourself.

Your values might be freedom, family, career, job satisfaction,
making a difference, doing the right thing, helping others, making
the most of your talents, generosity, kindness – many things! Revisit
your list of non-negotiables or deal-breakers, if that helps.

Education

"Education breeds confidence. Confidence breeds hope. Hope breeds peace." ~ **Confucius**

There's never any reason to stay stuck or feel depressed if you keep curious about the world, and keep learning. These days it's so easy to learn. If you can't travel, you can sign up to a course at a local learning centre, or visit a library, or download e-books, or study e-courses at home or on your commute into work. Many of these options are free.

After a break-up, it can be easy to lose interest in our own life and future, but learning something new will breathe optimism and energy back into your brain and soul and give you something constructive to aim towards. It will also introduce you to new people and ideas and raise your self-esteem – something that seems to plummet when we find ourselves on our own again.

Sign up for a course in a subject you've always wanted to learn about or spend time on – now is the perfect time to do it. It will also be a great way of meeting new people and taking you out of yourself. Online courses are good because they offer a convenient method of learning, and you can still connect with fellow students online. But in-person courses are more sociable.

You might also like to read up on the psychology of separation and relationships. This will arm you with the facts to help you get over someone and into a better, healthier mindset. Also, it's easier to process something once we start learning about it. There's a reading list in the resources section of this book to get you started.

Checklist and Mantras

1. I feel happier and more hopeful about my life.
2. I have a much better idea of where I'm going and how I'm going to get there.
3. I have more clarity about what I want.
4. I feel more confident.
5. I feel more inspired.
6. I've planned a fun week ahead doing things I love, with people who make me happy.

CHAPTER TEN

MOVING ON

"Life shrinks or expands in proportion to one's courage."
~ Anais Nin

EXERCISE: Confidence

The quickest way to change how you feel is to change what you do with your body. When we've just broken up with someone, our confidence can take a nosedive. Instead of letting it slip further into the abyss, this exercise can help it skyrocket instead.

1. Start by standing up straight. Imagine a thin golden thread pulling you up through the top of your head. Take a deep breath in and let your shoulders relax.

2. Close your eyes and visualise a highly confident, successful person standing in front of you now. This might be someone you know, it might be a celebrity, or it might be an imaginary person.

3. Think about how they look, walk, dress, talk and act towards others. If it helps, watch videos online of supremely confident people and study how they move and talk.

4. Now, imagine you have to play the part of that person, as you would a character in a film. You have to take on their personality and behaviour. Practice being them for a while. Walk around the room how they would walk around a room. Really enjoy *being* them for a while. Play-acting and modelling is something we do as children but we stop when we're adults. But it can be very effective for changing our state instantly, and rehearsing who we want to be. The important thing is to really *feel* the way this confident person does.

5. Stay in this role as long as you can. If you like, you can create a switch or anchor so you can access this feeling easily in future. Your switch might be pressing your finger and

thumb together, lightly pulling on your ear, or clicking your fingers – anything. My confidence switch is making a fist. But do whatever works for you.

Now open your eyes and take a deep breath. Repeat the exercise once more, and as many times as possible throughout the week. The more you do it, the more confident you will feel. Confidence will become your new habit.

EXERCISE: Compliments

1. Write down any compliments you can remember people paying you in the past. It can be anything – something you did, something you said, the way you looked, anything – from any time in your life. The more things you can think of, the better.

2. Now, stand in front of the mirror and close your eyes. Take a deep breath and relax.

3. Visualise someone you know and love standing in front of you now. If you can't think of anyone, imagine someone you like and respect standing in front of you.

4. Take one of your compliments and imagine this person saying it to you with all their heart. Really take it on board and believe it. Take it into your heart and let it percolate around.

5. Now open your eyes and look in the mirror and smile. See yourself as that special person sees you. Say thank you for being you. While you're doing this, press your thumb and middle finger together, or whatever you decided for your confidence anchor. This will add to your feel-good switch that you can fire off any time you need it.

6. Let go and open your eyes. Take a deep breath and look around the room.

7. Do this with as many compliments as you can. From now on, make a note of anything nice anyone says to you, even if it's a stranger in the street. Keep track of all your compliments and build a stockpile of confidence-boosters to draw on whenever you're feeling down. Practice this exercise every morning and evening.

EXERCISE: Ideal Partner

Write a profile of your imaginary ideal partner. Have some fun with this. If there are some criteria that are similar to your ex, that's OK, but don't dwell on them, or use it as a reason to get back together. If in doubt, revisit your list of things that annoyed you. The point here is to expand your mind beyond your current circumstances, and imagine someone who's going to treat you right and make you happy – ie, not your ex.

If you don't think you can get someone as good as your ex, or if they still represent the pinnacle of amazingness in your mind, you're going to have to work doubly hard on this exercise. Because, let me tell you, there are plenty of potential life partners out there for you. And now is the time to imagine who they are or where they might be. I'm not suggesting you jump into a new relationship straight away. But there's nothing wrong with getting clear on what you want, and setting yourself up for meeting someone new when the time is right.

Writing a profile of your ideal partner will reprogram your subconscious mind, and send strong signals about what you want. One of the benefits of doing yoga and meditation daily is you'll start to only attract positive, healthy people to you. Everyone else seems to fall away or stop bothering you. If you believe in the law of attraction, all this is a powerful way to manifest the right person. If not, then what's the harm in trying? Writing out your ideal anything will at least clarify what you want in life. No bad thing.

Intuition

"The power of 'the eye of the heart,' which produces insight, is vastly superior to the power of thought, which produces opinions." ~ E.F. Schumacher, British economic theorist and philosopher

"What is essential is invisible to the eye." ~ The Little Prince, Antoine de Saint-Exupéry

Our thoughts are usually egoic in nature, which means they're fear-based and mostly concerned with keeping us alive. Our intuition, on the other hand, is connected to our higher self and concerned with our greater good.

Our intuition always has our best interests at heart. It knows the right answer. Whether we choose to listen to it or not, is another matter. But I'm sure you can recall times when you didn't listen, and remember what happened next.

Always pay close attention to your intuition when you meet someone for the first time. It will give you a big clue as to who that person is and how the relationship is going to go. If you listen to your inner voice, and act on it, it can save you a lot of heartache later down the line.

Also pay close attention to the way someone behaves, not just what they say. Actions speak far louder than words. What did you learn about your ex when you first met them? What did your intuition tell you? Was it right? Don't be afraid to trust your inner voice, and walk away from anyone or anything that doesn't feel right. Our intuition is our own, valuable built-in safety mechanism to guide us to safety and happiness. Trust it.

Checklist and Mantras

1. I feel more confident.
2. I have an idea of what my ideal partner looks like.
3. I notice and remember when people compliment me.
4. I trust my intuition to keep me safe and direct me to the things that are right.

The Heartbreak Cure: *Express Version!*

Don't have time to work through all the exercises in this book? Try this 15-minute, quick-fix version instead. Repeat as often as you like.

1. Take a few deep breaths and relax. Recall five incidences when your ex did or said something to offend or upset you. Spend a few minutes running through each memory back-to-back in your mind. Concentrate on how you felt at the time. See what you saw, hear what you heard, feel what you felt as if it were happening all over again. Magnify this feeling. What are you saying to yourself about them in your mind? Run through all five memories a few more times. Now relax. Make all the movies grey, and turn down the sound. Now make them small and throw them away.

2. Imagine your ex in your mind now. What do they look like? Think of your ex's worst physical feature and amplify it in your mind. Make them look really ugly. Take all the colour out of the picture and make it really small. Shrink it to the size of a dot and throw it away. Do this with a few different memories of your ex. Make them grey then very small then throw them away.

3. Take two big deep breaths, and as you breathe out, say to yourself "release" and imagine letting go of anything that doesn't serve you.

4. Run through the tapping sequence as outlined above.

5. Write down all the things you want to achieve in your life and who you want to do them with. The more detailed, the better.

6. Organise to do something or see someone that makes you really, really happy in the next 24 hours.

7. Think of something really funny that always makes you laugh.

8. Put on some music that makes you really happy. Jump up and down, shake out your whole body, then stand in the power pose and imagine your life rocketing into mind-blowing amazingness in the next few months, now you are free to do whatever you want!

Action Plan For The Next 30 Days

1. Stay strong – keep a clear head on your shoulders. Stay away from your ex (until you feel 150% rock solid and emotionally detached)
2. Take daily action on your dreams and goals
3. Exercise daily, eat healthily and get plenty of good-quality sleep. Exercise and sleep as much as you can
4. Practice yoga as often as you can
5. Practice deep breathing at least twice a day, morning and night
6. Practice the visualisations to remove negativity at least twice a day, morning and night
7. Continually monitor negative thoughts in your thought journal, and actively practice replacing them with positive ones
8. Whenever you're feeling overwhelmed, angry, or anxious, practice tapping, shaking it out, power pose, deep breathing or Reiki. Repeat the Reiki principles morning and night
9. Continue to do your gratitude/appreciation journal every night
10. Keep note of any compliments paid to you
11. Continue to sever ties in your mind, until you feel relief, neutrality and detachment
12. If you catch yourself thinking of your ex, stop and do something else. Get your mood board or vision board out and focus on that instead. Go for a walk or run. Remind yourself why you're not with that person anymore
13. Reread this book as many times as you can

Conclusion

That's it! Congratulations. You've come very far, and done lots of hard work and I'm very proud of you! Hopefully by now your ex should be out of your system, and you'll be feeling much healthier and happier in yourself. You should be able to think about the past and your old relationship with detachment and clarity. In time, you'll be able to look back with fondness, but for now, just keep focused on yourself and you future until the past fades away of its own accord.

Your mind will continue to process everything, especially at night in your dreams. All you need to do is stick to the action plan, and stay as positive and healthy as you can. Most importantly, keep taking good care of yourself. You are the most important thing now!

Remember, you are your own soul mate/partner/best friend, and nobody can top that. And when the right person comes along, you will be ready for them, and can take it slow. See how they behave rather than rushing into something, just to fill a void. Take the time now to lay the foundations for a healthy, happy relationship. Always remember to follow your heart and trust your intuition. They're there to guide you.

Remember to fill your life with things that are meaningful to you. Things that make *you* happy. Things you care about. Feed your own soul. Find a job you love, surround yourself with happy people, learn new skills, create stuff, spend time on your own, get to know yourself. And, more importantly, *hold on to this stuff!* The more you fill your own life, the less you'll need someone else to do it for you. If someone amazing does come along, great. But that's not your sole reason for existence. They're the icing on the cake, not the cake itself.

Don't give yourself away for free. Don't give away your power. Make people work for your affection and time. Make them come to you and treat you right. Because, without wanting to sound like a shampoo commercial, you are worth it.

People will test you, and push your boundaries – it's human nature – but if you remain grounded and centred, you won't be taken for a ride. You will keep your cool. You will hold the reins.

Be the sort of person who is happy in their own skin. Be in a relationship because you *choose* to be, not because you *need* to be. Build the sort of life and confidence that means you can walk away at any time. Build in your own security measures so you're never relying on someone 100%.

The happier and more content you are, the less needy you'll be, and therefore the less fragile and dysfunctional the relationship will be. Plus, independence is a very attractive quality. When you are happy and fulfilled in yourself, you exude self-respect and self-confidence. You place a high value on yourself and your time, which in turn will make people value you more. Life is a self-fulfilling prophecy. What you put out, you get back.

If you put all your eggs in one basket, you're asking for trouble. So spread your bets, have contingency plans, have lots of friends and interests, build strong foundations for yourself, stay focused on your dreams, and future-proof your own life. Then you'll feel secure and confident, and never be left high and dry ever again.

I sincerely hope this book has helped you. No more languishing for days, weeks, months or (heaven forbid) years. If you've enjoyed it, please do leave me an honest review. Reviews mean the world to writers, and they help others make informed choices on the books they buy. I've also released a Heartbreak Cure journal, so you can write down all your thoughts or answers to the exercises from this book.

And you can now take *The Heartbreak Cure* as an online course, either on Udemy: www.udemy.com/share/102ei4AkETd1dURXg=/ or as a full-blown course on Thinkific: https://millercoaching.thinkific.com/courses/the-heartbreak-cure or

If you would like more personalised help, you can book a one-to-one session with me – just email me on acmillerbooks@gmail.com to set this up.

I wish you all the health, happiness, peace, strength, success and – of course – love in the world.

Thank you for being here.

Love,

A.C Miller

acmillerbooks@gmail.com
https://acmillerbooks.wordpress.com/

RESOURCES

The Ultimate Mix Tape for Break-Ups and Breakdowns

Whenever heartache comes a-knocking, slam these tunes on, crank up the volume, and I defy you not to feel better. I mean, doesn't it help just a little to know that J-Lo and Beyoncé get heartbroken? Altogether now: "We Are Never Ever Getting Back Together... To the left, to the left!"

1. Destiny's Child "Independent Woman" and "Survivor"
2. "Somebody That I Used to Know" by Gotye featuring Kimbra
3. "Walk On By" by Dionne Warwick
4. "We Are Never Ever Getting Back Together" by Taylor Swift
5. "Forget You" by Cee Lo Green
6. "I Will Survive" by Gloria Gaynor
7. "Go Your Own Way" by Fleetwood Mac
8. "You Oughta Know" by Alanis Morissette
9. "Fuck You Right Back" by Frankee
10. "The Otherside" by Breaks-Co-Op
11. "Don't Speak" by No Doubt
12. "Since U Been Gone" by Kelly Clarkson
13. "Ain't It Funny" by Jennifer Lopez

14. "Irreplaceable" and "Me, Myself & I" by Beyonce
15. "I Learned the Hard Way" by Sharon Jones & the Dap-Kings
16. "Someone Like You" by Adele
17. "Two Medicines" by The Dodos
18. [Add your own here]
19.
20.
21.
22.
23.
24.
25.

Suggested reading

Calling In "The One" by Katherine Woodward Thomas
Committed by Elizabeth Gilbert
F**k It: The Ultimate Spiritual Way by John C. Parkin
He's Just Not That Into You by Greg Behrendt and Liz Tuccillo
How to Have a Healthy Divorce: A Relate Guide by Paula Hall
I Can Mend Your Broken Heart by Hugh Willbourn and Paul McKenna
I Heart Me: The Science of Self Love by David R. Hamilton
It's Called a Breakup Because It's Broken by Greg Behrendt and Amiira Ruotola-Behrendt
Loving Yourself Loving Another: The Importance of Self-esteem for Successful Relationships (Relate Guides) by Julia Cole
Moving on: Breaking Up without Breaking Down (Relate Relationships) by Suzie Hayman
Moving On: Dump Your Relationship Baggage and Make Room for the Love of your Life by John W. James and Russell Friedman
Sacred Space: Enhancing the Energy of Your Home and Office by Denise Linn
Switchword Manifestation by Doron Alon
Tapping the Healer Within by Roger Callahan
The Art of Loving by Erich Fromm
The Grief Recovery Handbook by John W. James and Russell Friedman
The Power of Full Engagement by James Loehr
The Secret of Perfect Living by James Mangan

The Tao of Dating: The Smart Woman's Guide to Being Absolutely Irresistible by Ali Binazir MD
You Can Heal Your Life by Louise Hay
What Is Smudging: A Beginner's Guide To The Essentials by C.J Todd
Why Men Love Bitches by Sherry Argov

Online Resources

Relate: http://www.relate.org.uk/
Samaritans: http://www.samaritans.org/
The Grief Recovery Method:
http://www.griefrecoverymethod.co.uk/
The Science Behind Yoga: http://upliftconnect.com/yoga-and-stress/
Roger Callahan and TFT:
http://www.rogercallahan.com/callahan.php

Thought Journal Template

The thought	Emotions caused by the thought	Alternative ways of thinking about the situation

Abraham Maslow's Hierarchy of Needs

Abraham Maslow's hierarchy of needs, with the most important human needs at the bottom

NOTES

INDEX

Introduction   9

The Aim of This Book   14

What You Will Need   16

What You Can Expect To Feel By The End   17

The Ground Rules   18
    Rule No.1   19
    Rule No.2   22

The Techniques   24

The Pattern of a Break-Up   25

Your Tools   28

Subconscious   30

Habits   32

Beliefs   33

Associations   35

Hope   37

Imagination   39

Tapping   42

Music   46

Rhythm   48

Chemical Trance   **49**

Declaration of Intent   **54**

CHAPTER ONE: AUDIT   **55**

   EXERCISE: The Good, The Bad, and The Ugly   56

   EXERCISE: Old Exes – Where Are They Now?   58

CHAPTER TWO: REMOVE REMINDERS   **62**

   EXERCISE: Break-Up Box   63

   EXERCISE: Book a Trip   65

   EXERCISE: Change Your Surroundings   68

   EXERCISE: Change Your Appearance   69

   EXERCISE: Get What You Want   70

Dealing with rejection   **73**

   EXERCISE: Turn the Tables   74

   Checklist and Mantras   75

CHAPTER THREE: SEVER TIES   **76**

   EXERCISE: Bad Memories   80

     OPTIONAL EXTRA 1:   82

     OPTIONAL EXTRA 2:   83

   EXERCISE: Closing the Loop   84

     OPTIONAL EXTRA   86

   EXERCISE: Uglify Your Ex   87

   EXERCISE: Lookalikes   89

   EXERCISE: See Your Relationship In
The Third Person   90

   EXERCISE: Let Go   91

   EMERGENCY EXERCISE:
For When You Can't Stop Thinking Of Your Ex   94

   Checklist and mantras   95

CHAPTER FOUR: DETOX   **96**

   EXERCISE: Detox The Body   98

   EXERCISE: Surrender Box   101

   EXERCISE: Detox The Mind   103

   EXERCISE: Monitoring Negative Thoughts   105

   EXERCISE: Dealing With Haters   108

   EXERCISE: Someone Else's Mouth   111

   EXERCISE: Bla-Bla   112

   EXERCISE: Small Pictures   113

   EXERCISE: Eyes   115

   EXERCISE: Breath   117

     Breathing Exercise 1   118

     Breathing Exercise 2   119

   Checklist and Mantras   121

CHAPTER FIVE: SELF CARE   **122**

Yoga   **125**

   EXERCISE: Mantras and Affirmations   126

   EXERCISE: Reiki   128

   Checklist and Mantras   130

CHAPTER SIX: FEEL BETTER NOW   **131**

   EXERCISE: Reframing   135

   Exercise: Rewrite Your Relationship   137

   EXERCISE: Mood Board   139

   EXERCISE: Vision Board   140

   EXERCISE: Gratitude Journal   141

   Checklist and Mantras   143

CHAPTER SEVEN: GET PHYSICAL   **144**

   EXERCISE: Power Pose   147

EXERCISE: Shake It Out 148

EXERCISE: Balance and Twist 149

EXERCISE: Anger 150

   Some Ways to Deal With Anger 152

EXERCISE: Chi Kung 155

Checklist and Mantras 157

CHAPTER EIGHT: LEARN THE LESSONS **158**

EXERCISE: Benefit Finding 161

Investment and sacrifice **162**

EXERCISE: Non-Negotiables and Deal-Breakers 164

EXERCISE: Why You Got Into The Relationship 165

The Role of Parents **168**

EXERCISE: Re-imagining Parents 170

EXERCISE: Forgiveness 172

Checklist and Mantras 176

CHAPTER NINE: CREATE A COMPELLING FUTURE .. **177**

EXERCISE: Top 10 180

EXERCISE: In Five Years 183

EXERCISE: This Time Next Year 184

EXERCISE: Good Stuff 185

EXERCISE: Values 186

Education **187**

Checklist and Mantras 189

CHAPTER TEN: MOVING ON **190**

EXERCISE: Confidence 192

EXERCISE: Compliments 194

EXERCISE: Ideal Partner 196

Intuition   **197**
   Checklist and Mantras   199

The Heartbreak Cure: Express Version!   **200**

Action Plan For The Next 30 Days   **202**

Conclusion   **203**

RESOURCES   **206**
   The Ultimate Mix Tape for Break-Ups
   and Breakdowns   206

Suggested reading   **208**

Online Resources   **210**
   Thought Journal Template   211
   Abraham Maslow's Hierarchy of Needs   212

ABOUT A.C MILLER

A.C Miller is a health, psychology and wellbeing writer based in
London, England.

You can keep in touch with A.C Miller and receive updates on any
new releases
by following this link.

Alternatively, you can email acmillerbooks@gmail.com and request
to be added to the mailing list. I promise to keep all your details
confidential and I never spam.

Lightning Source UK Ltd.
Milton Keynes UK
UKHW021836211021
392611UK00006B/579